Samuel French Acting Edition

Barbarians

Book by
Maxim Gorky

Translated by
Kitty Hunter Blair,
Jeremy Brooks &
Michael Weller

SAMUELFRENCH.COM   SAMUELFRENCH.CO.UK

Copyright © 1982 by Kitty Hunter Blair, Jeremy Brooks & Michael Weller
All Rights Reserved

BARBARIANS is fully protected under the copyright laws of the United States of America, the British Commonwealth, including Canada, and all other countries of the Copyright Union. All rights, including professional and amateur stage productions, recitation, lecturing, public reading, motion picture, radio broadcasting, television and the rights of translation into foreign languages are strictly reserved.

ISBN 978-0-573-60658-8

www.SamuelFrench.com
www.SamuelFrench.co.uk

For Production Enquiries

United States and Canada
Info@SamuelFrench.com
1-866-598-8449

United Kingdom and Europe
Plays@SamuelFrench.co.uk
020-7255-4302

Each title is subject to availability from Samuel French, depending upon country of performance. Please be aware that *BARBARIANS* may not be licensed by Samuel French in your territory. Professional and amateur producers should contact the nearest Samuel French office or licensing partner to verify availability.

CAUTION: Professional and amateur producers are hereby warned that *BARBARIANS* is subject to a licensing fee. Publication of this play(s) does not imply availability for performance. Both amateurs and professionals considering a production are strongly advised to apply to Samuel French before starting rehearsals, advertising, or booking a theatre. A licensing fee must be paid whether the title(s) is presented for charity or gain and whether or not admission is charged. Professional/Stock licensing fees are quoted upon application to Samuel French.

No one shall make any changes in this title(s) for the purpose of production. No part of this book may be reproduced, stored in a retrieval system, or transmitted in any form, by any means, now known or yet to be invented, including mechanical, electronic, photocopying, recording, videotaping, or otherwise, without the prior written permission of the publisher. No one shall upload this title(s), or part of this title(s), to any social media websites.

For all enquiries regarding motion picture, television, and other media rights, please contact Samuel French.

Please refer to page 137 for further copyright information.

The action takes place in a small provincial Russian town in the early 1900's.

Act One

Ivakin's stall and garden on the outskirts of town.

Act Two

SCENE 1 – The garden of Tatyana Nikolayevna's house.
SCENE 2 – The same. Two months later.

Act Three

The sitting room in Tatyana Nikolayevna's house. Two months later.

BARBARIANS

Presented by the BAM Theater Company in the Helen Owen Carey Playhouse, at the Brooklyn Academy of Music, Brooklyn, New York, on April 10, 1980, with the following cast:

IVAKIN, *gardener and beekeeper* ...... Jerome Dempsey
YEFIM, *employed by Ivakin* .... Peter Phillips
MATVEY GOGIN, *a young peasant* .... Stephen Lang
DUNYA'S HUSBAND, *a person of
  indefinite profession* .... Frank Maraden
PAVLIN .... John Heffernan
MARIA IVANOVNA Vesyolkina,
  postmaster's daughter .... Sherry Steiner
DROBYAZGIN, Porphiry, *a Treasury
  clerk* .... Michael Hammond
PRITYKIN, Arkhip Fomich, *timber
  merchant* .... Gary Bayer
DR. MAKAROV .... Bill Moor
MONAKHOV, Mavriky Osipovich, *the local Tax
  Inspector* .... Brian Murry
LYDIA Pavlovna Bogayevskaya,
  Tatyana's niece .... Roxanne Hart
NADEZHDA Polikarpovna Monakhova, *wife of
  Monakhov* .... Sheila Allen
PELAGEYA Ivanovna Pritykina,
  wife of Pritykin .... Joan Pape
TATYANA NIKOLAYEVNA Bogayevskaya, *gentlewoman
  of property and Lydia's aunt* .... Avril Gentles
REDOZUBOV, VASSILY IVANOVICH,
  the Mayor .... Patrick Hines
STEPAN DANILOVICH LUKIN, *a student,
  Ivakin's nephew* .... Boyd Gaines

TSYGANOV, Sergi Nikolayich, *engineer* ......*John Seitz*
ANNA Fyodorovna Cherkoon, *wife*
    of Cherkoon ....*Marti Maraden*
STYOPA, *the Cherkoons's maid* ....*Anna Kluger Levine*
CHERKOON, Yegor Petrovich, *engineer*......*Jon Polito*
GRISHA, *Redozubov's son* ......*MichaelJohn McGann*
KATYA, *Redozubov's daughter* ....*Christine Estabrook*
CHIEF OF POLICE ....*Richard Jamieson*

DIRECTOR	*David Jones*
SET DESIGNER	*Andrew Jackness*
COSTUME DESIGNER	*Dunya Ramicova*
LIGHTING DESIGNER	*William Mintzer*
COMPOSER	*Bill Vanaver*
PRODUCTION STAGE MANAGER	*Stephen McCorkle*
ASSISTANT STAGE MANAGERS	*Ron Durbian* *Peter Glazer*

CHARACTERS

IVAKIN — gardener and beekeeper, age 50

YEFIM — worker employed by Ivakin, age 40

MATVEY Gogin — a young peasant, age 23

DUNYA'S HUSBAND — a person of indefinite profession, age 40

PAVLIN Savelyevich Golovastikov — age 60

VESYOLKINA, Maria Ivanovna — daughter of local postmaster, age 22

DROBYAZGIN, Porphiry — a Treasury clerk, age 25

PRITYKIN, Arkhip Fomich — timber merchant, age about 35

DR. MAKAROV — age 40

MONAKHOV, Mavriky Osipovich — the local Tax Inspector, age 40

LYDIA Pavlovna Bogayevskaya — age 28

NADIEZHDA Polikarpovna Monakhova — wife of Monakhov, age 28

PELAGEYA Ivanovna Pritykina — wife of Pritykin, age 45

BOGAYEVSKAYA, Tatyana Nikolayevna — a gentlewoman of property and Lydia's aunt, age 55

REDOZUBOV, Vassily Ivanovich — the Mayor, age 60

STEPAN Danilovich Lukin — student Ivakin's nephew, age 25

TSYGANOV, Sergei Nikolayich — a engineer, age 45

ANNA, Fyodorovna Cherkoon — wife of Cherkoon, age 23

STYOPA — the Cherkoons' maid, age 20

CHERKOON, Yegor Petrovich — engineer, age 23

GRISHA — Redozubov's son, age 20

KATYA — Redozubov's daughter, age 20

CHIEF OF POLICE — age 45

Barbarians

ACT ONE

A meadow on the bank of a river. On a rise across the river a small country town ringed with carefully tended gardens. Nearer the audience an orchard with a variety of trees, apple, cherry, lime, mountain ash, a few bee-hives and a round table dug into the ground, with benches. Around the orchard a dilapidated wattle fence with a pair of felt boots, and old jacket and a red shirt hung on its stakes. Skirting the fence is the road from the ferry landing to a mail-coach station. Inside the orchard to the R. the corner of a small house is visible. Attached to it is a lean-to which shelters a stall that sells bread, ring-shaped rolls, sunflower seeds, and home-brewed beer. L. of center just this side of the orchard fence stands a small thatched building. The garden continues to the L. beyond it.

A hot summer afternoon.

A corncrake can be heard in the distance occasionally, mingled with the doleful notes of a reedpipe. In the orchard, on the earth below his window sits IVAKIN, *a clean shaven man, bald, with a kindly, comical face. He plays his guitar with great concentration. Beside him sits* PAVLIN, *a fastidious little old man in a light, tight-fitting coat and peaked winter cap. On the window sill is a jug of beer and some mugs.* MATVEY, *a young man from the village is sitting on the ground by the fence, slowly chewing bread. From the direction of the station comes the lazy voice of an ill* WOMAN.

WOMAN. (*Off.*) Yefim. (*Silence.* DUNYA'S HUSBAND *appears to the* L., *a man of indefinite age, tattered and timid. Again, the woman's cry. Off.*) . . . Yefim! Yefim!

IVAKIN. Hey, Yefim, she's calling you. (YEFIM *enters along the garden side of the fence.*)

YEFIM. I heard. (*To* MATVEY.) What are you doing here?

MATVEY. Nothing. Just . . . sitting.

WOMAN. (*Off, irritated.*) Yo. Yefim!!!!!

IVAKIN. What's the matter, Yefim, you deaf?

YEFIM. (*Calls.*) I'm coming, damnit. (*To* MATVEY.) You got no business here. Go away. (YEFIM *takes his red shirt off the fence.* DUNYA'S HUSBAND *coughs and bows to him.*) Ah, so you're here, too. What do you want?

DUNYA'S HUSBAND. Just back from the monastery, Yefim Mitrich.

YEFIM. So they didn't want you, either. Monks and beggars, birds of a feather. To hell with all of you.

WOMAN. (*Off.*) Yefim!!!

IVAKIN. Better move it, my friend. (YEFIM *starts out.*) (*To* PAVLIN.) Likes to boss people around.

PAVLIN. Everybody likes to do that.

IVAKIN. Except the people that get it. Who wants to be yelled at for nothing.

PAVLIN. A little discipline never hurt. It doesn't seem to matter what you do, no one's ever satisfied.

IVAKIN. Now this little waltz, you can play it in a whole different style . . . listen.

DUNYA'S HUSBAND. Dear Lord, the man curses

everybody, saints and sinners, doesn't matter to him. And what for? I didn't do anything.

MATVEY. Christ it's hot.

DUNYA'S HUSBAND. I'm hot, too, but I suffer in silence. He thinks he can yell at everyone just because he has food in his stomach. He has no right. That looks like excellent bread.

MATVEY. It's all right.

DUNYA'S HUSBAND. Country-baked, I bet. Looks like it. They know how to make bread out in the villages, that's the truth.

MATVEY. When they can get flour they know how to make it. But I bought this from Ivakin.

DUNYA'S HUSBAND. Did you? Well, it smells like the real thing. I wouldn't mind sampling a piece myself.

MATVEY. There's not enough for me. (DUNYA'S HUSBAND *sighs, moves his lips.*)

IVAKIN. There, you see. And you can play it even slower.

PAVLIN. Did you say it's called the Waltz of the Mad Priest?

IVAKIN. That's the title.

PAVLIN. That's not good. It suggests a definite yielding to temptation and a disrespect for the calling of the church.

IVAKIN. There you go, criticising again. Why do you always look at the bad side of things, Pavlin?

PAVLIN. That's not fair. You know very well that my heart is humble. It's just I have a restless mind.

IVAKIN. What you have is an unpleasant personality. That's why people don't like you.

PAVLIN. I know what they say. I won't let it stop me from speaking out. I cry not when the mob persecutes me, I serve only one master; the truth, the whole truth and nothing but the truth.

IVAKIN. You can afford to. Nice little house, nice chunk of land, nice pile of money stashed away. (*Voices heard off,* L. IVAKIN *looks in that direction.*) Here comes that girl, the postmaster's daughter.

PAVLIN. She's a most shameless creature. A bitter fate awaits her. (DROBYAZGIN *and* VESYOLKINA *enter.*)

VESYOLKINA. I'm telling you, she was married to an engineer . . . she *was*.

DROBYAZGIN. Maria Ivanovna, I can't believe the things you say sometimes. Why don't you look at the facts.

VESYOLKINA. I see what I see and I know what I know.

DROBYAZGIN. Well, the facts are, a. Lydia Pavlovna's husband was not an engineer, he was the foreman of a licorice factory and b. she didn't throw him out at all, he died, he choked to death on a fish-bone.

VESYOLKINA. And I say she threw him out.

DROBYAZGIN. You're so incredibly cynical. You shouldn't be, you know. You don't look like a cynical person.

VESYOLKINA. She threw him out.

DROBYAZGIN. She did no such thing. I know the facts. I work in the Department of Finance. We hear everything about everything there. . . .

VESYOLKINA. Well, I work in the Post Office and we hear everything about everything and more, so there. And you can buy me a glass a beer. That's what you get for arguing. (IVAKIN, *taking this as an order, gets up and goes round the corner of the house.* PAVLIN *picks up* IVAKIN'S *guitar, looks inside it, touches the strings.*)

DROBYAZGIN. Of course I'll buy you a beer. But Lydia Pavlovna's a widow and you know it.

VESYOLKINA. Oh do I? You'll see. (*They exit towards the* R.)

DUNYA'S HUSBAND. (*Softly.*) Please . . . for the love of Christ, give me a piece, I'm starving.

MATVEY. You're weird! "I wouldn't mind sampling a piece", like you're a chef or something. Why didn't you come right out and ask?

DUNYA'S HUSBAND. Ask . . . just? . . . no, no, couldn't do that. (IVAKIN *returns with a jug of beer and two glasses which he puts on the table. He then stands looking at the town in the distance.*)

IVAKIN. Pavlin, look at the town. Beautiful, eh? Like a big pan full of fried eggs, eh?

PAVLIN. Just wait till they build the railway. That'll be the end of everything.

IVAKIN. There you go again, moan, moan, moan. What's wrong with the railroad?

PAVLIN. Strangers running all over town. Barbarians. You'll see. (*Re-enter* VESYOLKINA *and* DROBYAZGIN. *They sit at the table, drink beer and converse in low voices.* IVAKIN *and* PAVLIN *move off behind the corner of the house.*)

MATVEY. Who are you, anyway?

DUNYA'S HUSBAND. I'm from the town.

MATVEY. I thought all the townspeople were rich. What happened to you?

DUNYA'S HUSBAND. Ruined. Ruined. Dunya. My wife. Did me in. Took everything, my strength, even. Oh, she was all right at first. She's a pretty girl, very lively, you know. Then one day, out of the clear blue, 'I'm bored'. That's what she says. So she started to drink. I played along.

MATVEY. You drank?

DUNYA'S HUSBAND. What can you do? Went from

bad to worse. She took up with other men. Shameful. I beat her of course, went on beating her. She ran away. I had a daughter, fourteen years old. She ran away, too. Vanished. (*He is silent, in thought.*)

DROBYAZGIN. (*Loudly.*) Maria Ivanovna, you must stop saying these things. The doctor and Nadiezhda . . . it's impossible . . .

VESYOLKINA. Shh, not so loud.

MATVEY. Does she go for the men, too?

DUNYA'S HUSBAND. Who?

MATVEY. Your daughter?

DUNYA'S HUSBAND. How should I know? I don't even know where she is. Someone beat me up when I was drunk, this was later on, kicked me right in the heart. Never recovered. Still in pain. Can't work. Couldn't if I wanted to. I don't know how to do anything.

MATVEY. You're a mess, aren't you. How do you manage?

DUNYA'S HUSBAND. Day to day, that's all. Day to day. (DROBYAZGIN *jumps up.*)

DROBYAZGIN. No, no, I'm not going to listen any more. Isn't there anything in the world, that you hold sacred?

VESYOLKINA. Don't shout. You're acting like a lunatic.

DROBYAZGIN. But . . . I mean, Lydia Pavlovna and the Chief of Police. . . . !!!

VESYOLKINA. Shut up, sit down and drink your beer.

DUNYA'S HUSBAND. Today's the day the engineers arrive.

MATVEY. The railroad people?

DUNYA'S HUSBAND. That's it. Everywhere, everywhere they build their railroads, and still there's no place for a man to go.

MATVEY. At least there'll be some jobs. I wouldn't mind working for a change. (PAVLIN *appears in the orchard, approaches the table.* VESYOLKINA *sees him coming.*)

VESYOLKINA. (*Quietly.*) Here comes old grouchface.

DROBYAZGIN. Well, if it isn't the venerable sage himself. What's new in the world?

PAVLIN. Good health to you both.

DROBYAZGIN. Same to you.

PAVLIN. The Mayor just crossed the river. He's coming this way.

VESYOLKINA. He wants to meet the engineers, I bet. Imagine . . . going out of his way like that . . . and he's such a proud old man. (IVAKIN *enters, panting.*)

DROBYAZGIN. That he is. Ah, Ivakin. Hot, isn't it?

IVAKIN. Yes, it's very hot.

PAVLIN. You know what makes a person hot? Impatience. Now I'm not waiting for anyone so I'm not impatient, and since I'm not impatient I'm not hot.

IVAKIN. Look, the doctor's coming. And the tax collector's with him.

VESYOLKINA. We're not waiting for anyone. Are we waiting for anyone?

PAVLIN. I'm talking about Ivakin. He's waiting for his nephew. He's arriving with the engineers.

VESYOLKINA. The student?

IVAKIN. That's right. Look, Pritikin the timber merchant's coming, too. The whole town's on the move.

VESYOLKINA. A student. This is getting interesting. He's the first student we'll have ever had in the town.

DROBYAZGIN. Now you know that's not true, Maria Ivanovna. What about the statistician who shot himself.

VESYOLKINA. That doesn't count. He never got his degree.

PAVLIN. He was expelled for his political behavior,

and a good thing, too.

IVAKIN. (*Brusquely.*) And he shot himself because you informed on him. Anyone who'd do that to another person is a snake. (IVAKIN *moves away. The* DOCTOR, MONAKHOV *and* PRITIKIN *come along the road from the* L. MATVEY *stands and bows.* DUNYA'S HUSBAND *slips away quietly.*)

PRITYKIN. Well, each to his own and one man's meat, but I must say in all honesty, I don't see it, doctor, I just don't understand what pleasure you can possibly find in catching fish.

DR. MAKAROV. (*Morosely.*) For one thing, fish don't talk.

MONAKHOV. Pritikin, your problem is you don't understand anything about anything. Swimming in the summer, a steaming bath in the winter, that's the extent of your spiritual understanding. (PAVLIN *goes to the bank and sits by the fence.*)

PRITYKIN. Cleanliness is next to godliness, you know.

DROBYAZGIN. (*Shouts.*) We got here ahead of you. (*The* DOCTOR *stops by the fence.*)

DR. MAKAROV. Order some beer, Drobyazgin.

DROBYAZGIN. (*Shouts.*) Ivakin, beer over here . . . lots of it . . . and make sure it's good and cold.

PRITYKIN. One pleasure I understand is winning at cards.

MONAKHOV. I won't argue with that.

PRITYKIN. And music, there's another thing. Ah, when those trumpets start to play I feel like an entire army marching into battle. (*The* DOCTOR *smiles grimly at* MONAKHOV.)

DR. MAKAROV. Here comes the flattery. (DROBYAZGIN *goes to the fence and listens attentively, wanting to join in the conversation but too slow to find an open-*

ing. VESYOLKINA *moves farther back, gazes at the town and hums a tune to herself.*)

PRITYKIN. I don't have to flatter him. He knows it's true. His name will go down in the annals of this town . . . "Mavriky Osipovich, the man who taught our firemen to play music."

MONAKHOV. Well, I don't know about that, but it wasn't easy, I can tell you. I'd've had an easier time teaching walruses to sing opera.

PRITYKIN. Nowadays, when I see a samovar, Mavriky Osipovich, I think of you.

DR. MAKAROV. (*Unsmiling.*) Did you know you looked like a samovar? (DROBYAZGIN *laughs.*)

PRITYKIN. No, no. I mean the brass. A samovar is brass, like trumpets. That's what reminds me of you, brass of any kind.

DR. MAKAROV. He's going to strangle you to death with all this flattery.

PRITYKIN. I'm talking about music . . . your work with music.

MONAKHOV. What's all this twittering for, anyway. What are you after?

PRITYKIN. I'm after nothing. If I'm twittering I'm doing so in the spirit of the lark, just for my own pleasure. The doctor here just likes to sneer because he's bad tempered and doesn't like anything in the world. Except fish. (MONAKHOV *looks off to one side.*)

MONAKHOV. The ladies seem a little tired. They're moving like snails, look.

DROBYAZGIN. It's hard on Tatyana Nikolayevna. She's old and she has to carry all that weight with her.

IVAKIN. You have some beer here.

DR. MAKAROV. Am I going to walk around? No, I am not. (*The* DOCTOR *steps over the fence.*)

MONAKHOV. Tatyana's neice doesn't seem to care for our company, very much.

DROBYAZGIN. She's a society lady. She thinks she's better than us.

PRITYKIN. She rides a horse very nicely.

MONAKHOV. Yes, that she can do, all right.

PRITYKIN. You know what we forgot? I mean before, we were talking about the pleasures of life and we left out the fair sex. Isn't that the pleasantest thing of all? I'm not talking about my wife, of course.

MONAKHOV. (*Laughs.*) Pritikin, Pritikin . . . let's go, the beer's getting warm. (MONAKHOV *and* PRITIKIN *walk around the fence.*)

PRITYKIN. It's getting late, isn't it? The mail coach should be here any minute now. We'll see what these engineers are like at last.

MONAKHOV. Yes, that should be interesting. One thing you can bet on, they'll go for a game of cards.

PRITYKIN. And a drink or two, eh? (*They pick up their glasses and drift away. Enter* DUNYA'S HUSBAND.)

MATVEY. Have they all come here just to meet the engineers?

DUNYA'S HUSBAND. They were in the next village, at the fair. But engineers are engineers. Everybody wants to be the first to know them. Important people. That's how they do things. (LYDIA IVANOVNA *enters from the* R. *She is dressed in riding clothes, with a whip.*)

LYDIA. Would one of you be kind enough to look after my horse. I'll pay you.

MATVEY. I'll do it.

LYDIA. Thank you so much. (*She goes off to the* R.)

MATVEY. Look at that!

DUNYA'S HUSBAND. (*Irritable and envious.*) If you hadn't been here. It could be me looking after that horse right now.

MATVEY. You had your chance.

DUNYA'S HUSBAND. Listen, if she gives you a good tip, let me have five copeks, would you, would you do that?

MATVEY. What if I only get five? (*They both exit to* R. *The* DOCTOR *and* VESYOLKINA *are talking in the orchard.*)

DR. MAKAROV. (*Sullenly.*) When people are young, that's when they do things.

PAVLIN. (*Stands.*) You're forgetting about the holy fathers of the church. If I may make the observation, many of them were productive well into their later years.

DR. MAKAROV. So what?

PAVLIN. Well. Nothing. Just, they were. (*Enter* PELAGEYA PRITIKINA *and* NADIEZHDA POLIKARPOVNA, *the latter a very beautiful woman, tall with enormous, staring eyes.* TATYANA BOGAYEVSKAYA *is behind her.*)

NADIEZHDA. And then he says to her, "Alissa, my love for you moves inside of me like the ocean, and I am yours forever."

PELAGEYA. It's beautiful. You know all those wonderful love stories and they're all so beautiful, just like you dream about when you're a girl. Why don't our men know how to talk like that?

NADIEZHDA. (*Sitting on a log.*) Frenchmen are the most passionate and noble lovers, even if they are unfaithful. The Spaniards are the most fierce, even ferocious, and Italians, when they're in love they stand under your window all night and play the guitar.

BOGAYEVSKAYA. Nadiezhda, I'm beginning to think it was a big mistake that you ever learned to read.

NADIEZHDA. Maybe you've just reached an age where

none of this interests you any more, but I . . .
BOGAYEVSKAYA. But you . . . you talk and talk and talk.
PELAGEYA. Where's my husband?
BOGAYEVSKAYA. Isn't that Lydia's horse over there?
NADIEZHDA. Oh, would you introduce me to her?
BOGAYEVSKAYA. To the horse?
NADIEZHDA. No, to Lydia Pavlovna.
BOGAYEVSKAYA. You see, my dear, you've read a thousand novels and you can't even ask a simple question correctly.
NADIEZHDA. It doesn't matter. Nobody's perfect. (BOGAYEVSKAYA *goes off to the* R., *calling.*)
BOGAYEVSKAYA. Lydia . . . !
PELAGEYA. (*Softly.*) Dear oh dear, she's so rude to you.
NADIEZHDA. (*Calm.*) The gentry always talk that way to us ordinary folk. Look, here she comes. Isn't she beautiful! (BOGEVSKAYA *enters, followed by* LYDIA.)
BOGAYEVSKAYA. Lydia, dear, Nadiezhda Polikarpovna would like to meet you. (NADIEZHDA *curtsies.*) You see, she's even learned how to curtsy.
NADIEZHDA. I've seen you so often. You ride by our house every day on your horse and I admire the way you look. Like a countess or a marquise. It's very beautiful.
LYDIA. Yes, I've often seen your face in the window, and I return your admiration.
NADIEZHDA. Thank you. It's always nice to have another woman praise your beauty.
BOGAYEVSKAYA. She's not what you'd call shy.
DR. MAKAROV. (*Gloomily.*) Isn't it nicer to hear praise from a man than a woman.
NADIEZHDA. Well, of course it takes a man to fully appreciate a woman's beauty.
LYDIA. You seem so sure of yourself.

BARBARIANS

PRITYKIN. (*Shouts, off.*) Listen, can you hear the bells . . . they're coming! (*They listen. Sound of bells.*)

NADIEZHDA. (*To* LYDIA.) Aren't you longing to see what they're like?

LYDIA. Who? Shouldn't we be going home, Auntie?

NADIEZHDA. The engineers.

PRITYKIN. (*Rushes on.*) They're coming up the road.

LYDIA. (*To* NAD.) Why should I be dying to meet them?

BOGAYEVSKAYA. Let's wait a moment, my dear. I'm utterly exhausted.

NADIEZHDA. I've been awaiting their arrival as if it were my birthday.

PELAGEYA. What if they turn out to be old men?

LYDIA. (*Softly but urgently.*) Can we please go, Auntie. We look like some ridiculous reception committee. I feel absurd.

BOGAYEVSKAYA. Let's go into the orchard. I'd like a drink of something. Come along. (*All start out after her.*)

PRITYKIN. So they're here at last. It's quite interesting, isn't it, doctor.

DR. MAKAROV. Why? If they came all the way on foot, that might be interesting.

NADIEZHDA. Nonsense.

BOGAYEVSKAYA. Nadiezhda wants to see them galloping in on horseback, wearing armor and swords and long capes billowing out behind them. Come along. (*They all exit* R., *their slow conversation drowned in the sound of bells. From the* R. *appears* REDOZUBOV, *the Mayor, walking slowly, hands clasped behind his back. He is a gray-haired, severe old man with black, bushy eyebrows. He stops, listens to the noise from the mail station. Enter* PAVLIN, *taking his cap off deferentially long before they meet.*)

REDOZUBOV. Afternoon. You well?

PAVLIN. Thank you, very much so. And you, I trust the day finds you in the very best of health?

REDOZUBOV. Ask the doctor. They here yet?

PAVLIN. Indeed they are, the much awaited engineers. One's older than the other, has a moustache, seems he's had a sip or two on the way. The other one's younger and has remarkably red hair. There's a young lady, too, very beautiful and she has a maid with her, very dressed up. They came in two carriages. Three to be exact, but the last one's just luggage, except for that student, Ivakin's nephew.

REDOZUBOV. What's he doing with them?

PAVLIN. A victim of reduced circumstances. A traveller on the charity of others. (PRITIKIN *enters.*)

PRITYKIN. Good afternoon, Vassily Ivanich.

REDOZUBOV. (*Not shaking hands.*) Afternoon.

PRITYKIN. Have you come to welcome our illustrious guests?

REDOZUBOV. They're no use to me.

PRITYKIN. No, but in a general way, they'll be beneficial to the town, don't you think?

REDOZUBOV. Then let the town welcome them. (REDOZUBOV *walks off towards the station.*)

PRITYKIN. (*Softly.*) He doesn't mean that, does he?

PAVLIN. Of course not. He wants to get the contract for the railway ties.

PRITYKIN. He's a sly old fox. Now Pavlin, what you have to do is get to know the maid and see if you can find out what's what with them, just in general. Do you follow me?

PAVLIN. Of course. (*They exit towards the station. Enter* IVAKIN, *looking happy, with* STEPAN LUKIN, *the student.*)

STEPAN. So, how are things with you?

IVAKIN. I'm well, that's all I ask. But you look a little undercooked. How'd you manage to get yourself put in prison?

STEPAN. Couldn't avoid it. It's becoming a standard government requirement nowadays, like the draft. Don't worry, it doesn't mean anything. But, just to be on the safe side, I wouldn't mention it to anybody, all right, brother?

IVAKIN. Brother? Where'd you learn that? I'm not your brother, I'm your uncle.

STEPAN. You're not my uncle. You're just an old friend from childhood days. Look, I have the beginnings of a beard and your face is smooth as a baby's bottom.

IVAKIN. That's enough. Drink your beer and show a little respect for your elders. (PRITIKIN *rushes on.*) What's the trouble, Arkhip Fomich?

PRITYKIN. Nothing, they're just . . . (*Calls off.*) Hey, boy, over here. (MATVEY *enters.*) You know who I am, don't you. Run over to my house in town, tell them to send two carriages and a wagon for the luggage. Tell them to wait for me at the ferry landing. Can you remember that? Now get moving. (MATVEY *runs off, calling as he goes . . .*)

MATVEY. Hey, keep an eye on the horse for me, would you. Thanks. (PRITIKIN *runs off towards the station.*)

IVAKIN. Things are humming in the town of Verkhopolye.

STEPAN. What's with the ferry? What happened to the bridge?

IVAKIN. Had a storm a few months ago, whoosh, washed it right away.

STEPAN. Why doesn't the mayor do something about it?

IVAKIN. He's in no hurry. He owns the ferry. Say, are you in pretty tight with these engineer people?

STEPAN. I'm going to be working for them. So, what about yourself? How are the bees doing? And the guitar? And your fishing tackle?

IVAKIN. Fine, fine, everything's fine. (*Enter* DOCTOR, MONAKHOV, DROBYAZGIN, VESYOLKINA *in conversation.* IVAKIN *and* STEPAN *go off.* PAVLIN *appears, looks around and withdraws.*)

MONAKHOV. Did you see how that Pritikin moved in on them? Didn't waste any time introducing himself, what a weasel.

VESYOLKINA. Did you notice the younger one, Doctor? His hair's so red, it looks like a flaming torch.

DROBYAZGIN. And that woman has the most incredible eyes, did you notice that, Mavriky Osipovich?

VESYOLKINA. She does not. She has very ordinary eyes.

DROBYAZGIN. Well, I disagree. I think they're extraordinarily poetic.

MONAKHOV. It's not very tactful to praise one woman's beauty around another. You should know that by now.

DR. MAKAROV. It's disgusting. The way everyone's swarming around them like a bunch of mosquitos round a bonfire.

PRITYKIN. (*Off.*) Doctor, would you come here for a moment, please.

DR. MAKAROV. I'm busy.

PRITYKIN. (*Off.*) We need your professional assistance.

DR. MAKAROV. Damnit all. (DOCTOR *starts off.*)

MONAKHOV. Now you'll get to meet them too, lucky so and so. (VESYOLKINA *goes out after the* DOCTOR.

BARBARIANS

TSYGANOV *meets her as she exits. He is an elegantly dressed gentleman, slightly tipsy.* VESYOLKINA *is embarrassed and turns abruptly away from him.* TSYGANOV *raises an eyebrow in surprise.* DROBYAZGIN *bows to* TSYGANOV.)

TSYGANOV. (*Touching hat in return.*) Greetings. And to whom have I the honor?

DROBYAZGIN. (*Embarrassed.*) Porphiry . . . I mean, clerk, Department of Taxation, Porphiry Drobyazgin.

TSYGANOV. Ah, delighted. Tell me, does this charming town happen to have a hotel?

DROBYAZGIN. A very fine one . . . it even has a billiards room. And we have a high school for girls.

TSYGANOV. Really? A high school for girls. I'll probably have no immediate use for that. Do you have any such thing as a cab?

DROBYAZGIN. Three. We have three of them. They always wait in front of the church.

TSYGANOV. (*Blancing towards the town.*) I don't suppose they'd hear me if I called.

DROBYAZGIN. I shouldn't think so. After all, the town's two miles away.

TSYGANOV. Pity. (*Enter* DUNYA'S HUSBAND *from* L. PAVLIN *drifts on.*)

DUNYA'S HUSBAND. A little help, your excellency, alms for a poor, sick man. . . . (TSYGANOV *finds a coin.*)

TSYGANOV. Here you are. (DUNYA'S HUSBAND *shudders with delight.*)

DUNYA'S HUSBAND. God grant . . . bless you, sir, god bless you and yours. (DUNYA'S HUSBAND *exits.*)

TSYGANOV. Is he a drunk?

DROBYAZGIN. No, he really is poor and always sick, and his wife ran off and now he's . . . (MONAKHOV *comes over.*)

MONAKHOV. Excuse me, sir, if I may make so bold . . .
TSYGANOV. Feel free.
MONAKHOV. Mavriky Osipovich Monakhov. I'm the tax inspector for the district.
TSYGANOV. An honor. Sergei Nikolayich Tsyganov.
MONAKHOV. I feel it is my duty to inform you that the hotel here is filthy and overrun with bugs.
DROBYAZGIN. It's the shame of the town, a pesthole.
MONAKHOV. There is only one place in Verkhopolye for a gentleman to stay, and that's Madame Bogayevskaya's house. I'm sure I can arrange for her to rent it out. I'll take care of everyting. (MONAKHOV *leaves quickly.* ANNA FYODOROVNA *and* STYOPA *are entering.*)
TSYGANOV. (*After* MONAKHOV.) Just a moment, I don't really . . . that's very kind of you, but . . .
MONAKHOV. I'll be right back, leave everything to me. . . . (MONAKHOV *exits.*)
DROBYAZGIN. I'll get him back.
TSYGANOV. No, no, please. This is absurd. He's run off now.
ANNA. What's the matter?
TSYGANOV. The natives, they're smothering us with kindness. And, by the way, congratulations, there's no hotel in town.
ANNA. There seems to be difficulty even getting to the town. Some problem with the ferryboat. (TSYGANOV *beckons off.*)
TSYGANOV. Come here a moment, would you? (DUNYA'S HUSBAND *enters.*) Tell me, good sir, does this town have any local wonders that mustn't be missed while one is here?
DUNYA'S HUSBAND. Crayfish, sir. We have giant, enormous sized jumbo crayfish. (STYOPA *looks intently at* DUNYA'S HUSBAND.)

TSYGANOV. Do you? That's fascinating. But I should think they live more in the river than in the town itself, no?

DUNYA'S HUSBAND. Oh, yes, yes, always in the river. They're an animal that lives in the water.

STYOPA. (*Softly.*) Anna Fyodorovna . . . that man . . . it's him.

ANNA. Who?

STYOPA. My father. What'll I do now?

TSYGANOV. And in the town proper? Does anything interesting live there?

DUNYA'S HUSBAND. The firemen. They all play trumpets. Brass trumpets. The tax collector taught them how.

ANNA. Don't say anything, stand behind me.

TSYGANOV. Do they play very loudly . . . ?

DUNYA'S HUSBAND. They give it everything they've got. . . .

STYOPA. I'll go back to the mail coach. He hasn't seen me yet.

TSYGANOV. Well, so much for the pleasures of Verkhopolye. Thank you for your time. Here, take this.

DUNYA'S HUSBAND. Your excellency . . . (DUNYA'S HUSBAND *tries to kiss* TSYGANOV's *hand.*)

TSYGANOV. (*With revulsion.*) Please, that's not necessary. You can go now. (DUNYA'S HUSBAND *exits.* STYOPA *gazes after him.*)

STYOPA. A beggar . . . My father's a beggar. I told you he was bound to be here. I told you I shouldn't come, I told you not to bring me. I told you!

ANNA. Stop worrying, Styopa, he won't bother you while you're with us.

STYOPA. I'm afraid of him. He drove my mother mad.

TSYGANOV. And what's all this about, may I ask?

ANNA. That was her father.

TSYGANOV. Aha . . . now that's interesting.

ANNA. Is that all you can say? Go ahead, Styopa, go back to the coach.

TSYGANOV. We'll look after you, don't worry. (CHERKOON *shouts from offstage.*)

CHERKOON. Anna, Anna, come here. (TSYGANOV *looks in the direction of the shout.* ANNA *calls back to* CHERKOON.)

ANNA. What is it? I'm coming.

TSYGANOV. My God, I don't believe this. (TSYGANOV, *delighted, stretches out his arms towards* LYDIA PAVLOVNA, *who is approaching.*) Lydia Pavlovna, is it really you. This is incredible.

LYDIA. (*Entering.*) Dear old Sergei . . .

TSYGANOV. You, here in Terra del Fuego among the savages. How in the world? (VESYOLKINA *has returned to the garden. She walks alone, fanning her face with some flowers.* DROBYAZGIN *appears and they walk side by side, eavesdropping.*)

LYDIA. I've come to stay with my aunt. It's wonderful to see you again. Still fond of the ladies, I see.

TSYGANOV. Yes, but no luck yet. The first creature I met in this Siberia was a man, and he turns out to be the tax collector. (*Indicates* ANNA, *who is offstage.*)

LYDIA. And is that your wife?

TSYGANOV. Wife? I've never encumbered myself with such an extravagant possession, and I never shall. And your esteemed husband, where is he?

LYDIA. I haven't the faintest idea.

TSYGANOV. Well, bravo, a free woman at last. Are you?

VESYOLKINA. (*Overhearing this, to* DROBYAZGIN.) You see, what did I tell you?

LYDIA. You don't have to shout it to the whole world.

TSYGANOV. Have you met my partner yet? Georges, come here. (CHERKOON *approaches. To* LYDIA.) His manner is very bold and his hair is very red. (*To* CHERKOON.) Guess who I've run into here, Georges. You remember I told you about a certain young lady?

CHERKOON. Yes, I remember. In fact, he talked about you a great deal.

LYDIA. How nice. . . .

CHERKOON. But of course I never expected to meet you, expecially not in a dreary hole like this.

LYDIA. I take it you don't like the town?

CHERKOON. I don't like the countryside, period.

TSYGANOV. Scandal and excitement, that's what he likes. (NADIEZHDA *enters, stares at* CHERKOON. *She is motionless, face frozen like stone.*)

CHERKOON. Oh, yes, it's a pretty little scene. Charming little houses nestled among charming little trees. Somehow it makes you want to put your fists through it.

TSYGANOV. Why don't you introduce Lydia Pavlovna to your wife, Georges.

CHERKOON. Oh, certainly. May I?

LYDIA. I'd be delighted. But I think you're a bit hard on this poor little town.

TSYGANOV. You see, it takes a brute like this to make you appreciate the tender and sensitive soul of yours truly.

CHERKOON. When I see something I either like it or hate it.

TSYGANOV. See? A man without a single redeeming quality.

LYDIA. A man with no good qualities. Well, at least that's something definite. (TSYGANOV *notices* NADIEZHDA.)

CHERKOON. (*Calls.*) Anna. She'll probably love the view. She has a weakness for serene and peaceful landscapes.

LYDIA. I think a lot of people would find this spot quite poetic.

CHERKOON. Yes, everyone bloodless, idle and tired of living.

TSYGANOV. Who is that stately ship sailing towards us with your wife? (*Enter* ANNA *and* BOGAYEVSKAYA.)

LYDIA. That's my aunt.

CHERKOON. Anna, this is Lydia Pavlovna Bogayevskaya.

ANNA. How lovely to meet you.

BOGAYEVSKAYA. Well, everyone seems to have met. They've just rented the first floor of my house, Lydia.

ANNA. I'm glad it's all been taken care of so quickly . . . and conveniently.

TSYGANOV. Long live the architect of these wonderful arrangements, the one and only collector of taxes himself.

LYDIA. That's his wife in the orchard.

TSYGANOV. His wife? Her? Hmmmmm . . . (TSYGANOV *stares at* NEDIEZHDA.)

ANNA. I hope we're there soon. I'm exhausted.

BOGAYEVSKAYA. The ferry's on its way. (NADIEZHDA *walks off slowly.*)

CHERKOON. And look, horses waiting across the river already. What's that timber merchant's name. He's the one who arranged it.

BOGAYEVSKAYA. Pritikin. I'll go over in the skiff, Lydia. I want to make sure the house is ready for them.

ANNA. Please, don't worry about us.

CHERKOON. We're not completely helpless.

LYDIA. (*To* BOG.) Wait a moment. (*To* ANNA.) Do you ride?

ANNA. Heavens, no.

LYDIA. That's a pity. I was going to offer you my horse. There's a shallow place up the river where you can cross.

ANNA. That's very kind, but I'm afraid of horses. I saw one throw a little boy once. He was killed. Since then I've always had this feeling horses want to kill the person riding them. They're just waiting.

LYDIA. But you travel in a carriage. You're not afraid of that?

ANNA. It's different. There's a coachman between me and the horse.

CHERKOON. If that's supposed to be clever, Anna, I'm afraid it's rather feeble.

ANNA. I'm not trying to be clever.

TSYGANOV. (*To* LYDIA.) So, we meet again.

CHERKOON. I wish you would try sometimes, just for a change.

TSYGANOV. It's a miracle sent from above. . . .

LYDIA. Just an ordinary coincidence that proves the world's too small.

BOGAYEVSKAYA. (*To* ANNA.) Come over here, I want to show you our town. It's really quite charming. (*She takes* ANNA *to the fence.*)

TSYGANOV. You know you're more beautiful than ever. And your eyes, there's something different in your eyes.

LYDIA. Boredom, probably.

CHERKOON. Are you bored?

LYDIA. Life doesn't seem particularly interesting at the moment. (*Enter* REDOZUBOV *from the direction of the station. He approaches, coughs. He raises his hand to his hat to salute, then drops it quickly as if someone may have noticed this subservient gesture.*)

CHERKOON. I didn't expect that from you.

LYDIA. Why not?

CHERKOON. I don't know. I suppose I just didn't think you were the kind of person who'd see life that way.

LYDIA. Life is just people. I've seen plenty of them. After a while they seem more and more alike.

REDOZUBOV. I'm Vassily Ivanov Redozubov. I'm the mayor of this town. The mayor.

CHERKOON. Well?

REDOZUBOV. I want to speak to the head engineer. Which one of you's in charge?

TSYGANOV. We work together. We're equals, as in 'equality', if you can grasp the general concept.

REDOZUBOV. Will you be needing timber for the railway? I can supply you . . .

CHERKOON. (*Dryly.*) We'll be ready to discuss business next week, not before.

REDOZUBOV. (*Pause.*) I don't think you heard what I said.

CHERKOON. What did you say?

REDOZUBOV. I'm the mayor. I'm the head of the town.

CHERKOON. What's that got to do with us? We don't live here.

REDOZUBOV. (*Controlled.*) I am sixty-three years of age. I am the churchwarden. The entire town is under my control.

CHERKOON. Congratulations . . .

TSYGANOV. Your honor, please, our deepest respects to you and your town, and I assure you, as soon as we've had a chance to make ourselves comfortable here we'll look forward to availing ourselves of your many rare qualities. . . .

CHERKOON. But for now you can leave us alone. When we need you we'll send for you, thank you. (REDOZUBOV *measures* CHERKOON *with a murderous look, then walks away in silence.*)

BARBARIANS

ANNA. Why did you have to be so rude, Yegor? He's an old man, after all.

CHERKOON. He's an old bully is what he is. Head of the town. More like the other end of it. I know his kind. Arrogant, greedy, stubborn old horse's ass.

TSYGANOV. (*To* LYDIA.) So, how do you like my fiery friend here?

LYDIA. Not very much, I'm afraid.

BOGAYEVSKAYA. Come, Lydia, we should be starting back.

ANNA. It's just his manner. Underneath he's really . . .

CHERKOON. Gentle and sensitive and kind, is that what you were going to say? Because it's not true. I'm exactly what I seem to be.

LYDIA. Good-bye. Oh, dear, that man's handling the horse all wrong. (LYDIA *goes off quickly* R., *followed by* BOGAYEVSKAYA.)

BOGAYEVSKAYA. We'll be expecting you shortly.

TSYGANOV. Thank you very much indeed. We won't be long. Georges, you're looking at the town like Attila at the gates of Rome. Are you planning a conquest?

CHERKOON. God, what a dismal place. That woman . . . has she had lovers?

ANNA. Yegor, that's awful.

TSYGANOV. Georges, what a delicate way you have with words.

CHERKOON. (*To* ANNA.) What? You're shocked? Lots of women have lovers, didn't you know that?

ANNA. But people don't talk about it like that.

CHERKOON. *People* don't. *I* do. You think it's immoral?

ANNA. It's just not polite. It's vulgar.

CHERKOON. Really? I thought I might have offended your morals, but it's just a question of manners is it? Well, Sergei, has she?

TSYGANOV. Lovers? I don't like to think about it, frankly. And if anyone whispered something in my ear, I wouldn't believe them. (*Enter* PRITIKIN *and* DUNYA'S HUSBAND.)

PRITYKIN. Everything's ready if you'll just follow me. I've already had your luggage loaded on the ferry.

TSYGANOV. Well, you have been busy, haven't you.

PRITYKIN. Allow me . . .

TSYGANOV. Our deepest gratitude . . .

PRITYKIN. It's nothing, nothing at all. The very least we could do. Hospitality. A country welcome. . . .

TSYGANOV. You know you must be one of the five or six most wonderfully friendly men I've ever met. (*They exit together.*)

CHERKOON. Let's go. (ANNA *takes* CHERKOON'S *arm.*)

ANNA. Why so gloomy all of a sudden?

CHERKOON. I'm tired.

ANNA. That's not true. You're never tired.

CHERKOON. All right, then, I'm in love, is that better?

ANNA. (*Softly.*) Yegor, why do you always have to be so unpleasant? Why?

DUNYA'S HUSBAND. Your excellency . . .

CHERKOON. Get away from here . . . (ANNA *gives him a coin.*)

ANNA. Here, take this. (ANNA *and* CHERKOON *exit.* MATVEY *jumps up.*)

MATVEY. What did she give you?

DUNYA'S HUSBAND. Twenty copeks. That makes one rouble, twenty and the day is young.

MATVEY. Damn. Ten copeks, that's all I got.

PRITYKIN. (*Off, yelling.*) Hey, you there . . .

MATVEY. Coming. (MATVEY *goes.* PAVLIN *steps over the fence.*)

PAVLIN. Did you say one rouble twenty?

DUNYA'S HUSBAND. (*Timid.*) One-twenty, yes.

PAVLIN. Let me see. Hmmm, you're right. And you haven't lifted a finger for it. Mangey old gutter rat. Get out of here. Wait a moment. I'll tell you a little something. Do you want to hear this?

DUNYA'S HUSBAND. I haven't done anything Pavlin Savelich . . . (*Enter* REDOZUBOV.)

PAVLIN. What are you doing here? I told you to stop bothering everyone. Get moving. Go! (DUNYA'S HUSBAND *exits.*)

REDOZUBOV. They gone?

PAVLIN. Yes.

REDOZUBOV. You talked to their maid. What did you find out?

PAVLIN. All sorts of things. General conversation. She's not a highly talkative individual. I gave her a rouble at one point to see if that might loosen her tongue a little. . . .

REDOZUBOV. Damn fool. Now she can say you tried to bribe her.

PAVLIN. Ah, well, no, you see, Vassily Ivanich, what I mean precisely is that the rouble was never actually given to her, the actual giving of the rouble, the event itself happened in my mind, if you see what I mean. I found myself thinking, 'Perhaps if I gave her a rouble' and then I thought to myself, 'No, Pavlin, this girl is too spoiled, nothing will help. . . .' (REDOZUBOV *stares at the town, not listening.*) She's a runaway. Did you know that, Vassily Ivanich? Dunya's husband is her rightful father. I got it out of her. . . .

REDOZUBOV. (*Abruptly, severely.*) And did you know, Pavlin Savelich, the governor himself shakes hands with me. The governor.

PAVLIN. Of course he does. Everyone is very well

aware of that fact. (*Pause.* STEPAN'S *voice heard inside through the window.*)
  REDOZUBOV. Whose voice is that?
  PAVLIN. Ivakin's nephew, the student.
  REDOZUBOV. Shhhh, quiet. (*They listen. A dog is howling somewhere in the distance. A crowcall.*)
  STEPAN. (*Off.*) Just wait'll we finish pushing through with the railway. That'll burn all the old rot out of this town, you'll see. (STEPAN *laughs.*)
  REDOZUBOV. (*Softly.*) You hear that?
  PAVLIN. (*With conviction.*) It's nonsense.
  REDOZUBOV. Remember his words. Remember them. (*Beat. He exits, followed by* PAVLIN.)

CURTAIN

ACT TWO

The garden of TATIANA BOGAYEVSKAYA'S *house. A canvas awning is stretched out between the trees over a very large, simple, unpainted wooden table. To the* L. *is a house with a wide path leading up to it. At the end of the garden a fence.*

CHERKOON *is seated at the table with a pile of papers, maps and plans in front of him. Under the trees to the* L. *in a wicker chair sits* ANNA *with a book in her lap. She stretches.*

ANNA. Aren't you hot?
CHERKOON. Of course.
ANNA. Still no sign of Sergei. You always end up doing all the work, but you always want to be on the same jobs with him. Why?
CHERKOON. (*Without looking up.*) He knows far more than I do. He has experience.
ANNA. But he's so . . . degenerate.
CHERKOON. His morals don't interest me. His knowledge does.
ANNA. (*Pause.*) I wish everyone here wasn't so nosey. Always spying on us, eavesdropping. They're so naive.
CHERKOON. They're idiots, that's all.
ANNA. Look, there's someone in the next garden staring at us through the fence. I can see two eyes, gleaming at us.
CHERKOON. Who cares. Let them gleam. (*Enter* STEPAN.)

STEPAN. Well, I've hired that boy, Matvey Gogin. I have his papers here.

ANNA. I'll take them.

CHERKOON. Don't give them to her, she'll shove them away in a corner somewhere and forget where she put them. It's not funny, she always does that.

STEPAN. My god, the people here . . . They belong in a museum. It's enough to make you a pessimist for life.

CHERKOON. For a working man, pessimism is about as useful as white gloves. What's he like, this Matvey?

STEPAN. Not too stupid. See for yourself, here he comes. Do you need me here? (*Enter* MATVEY, *dressed more tidily than in the first act.*)

CHERKOON. No. (STEPAN *exits. To* MATVEY.) Well, what do you have to say for yourself?

MATVEY. I wanted to thank you for giving me this job, your excellency.

CHERKOON. I'm not an excellency. My name is Yegor Petrov and I'm a peasant by birth, just like yourself. You're going to work for me, I'm going to pay you for your labor. If you're lazy I'll fire you and if you cheat I'll have you run in. Do we understand each other?

MATVEY. Yes, you excel . . . Yegor Petrov, sir. I'll do my best. You won't be sorry.

CHERKOON. We'll see about that. You can go now. (MATVEY *hesitates, thinking.*)

MATVEY. Thank you, sir, thank you.

CHERKOON. (*Glancing up.*) What?

MATVEY. Sir?

CHERKOON. Nothing . . . go, go. (MATVEY *exits.*)

ANNA. Yegor, you're so hard on everyone.

CHERKOON. That's how they were with me. (*Pause.*)

ANNA. It was very kind of Tatiana Nikolayevna to rent us her house, don't you think? Do you like her?

BARBARIANS

CHERKOON. She's all right. I like her niece better.

ANNA. Why do you always have to tease me.

CHERKOON. Why do you let me get away with it. Make a scene. (GRISHA REDOZUBOV's *head appears over the fence.*)

ANNA. (*Alarmed.*) Look, Yegor, look.

CHERKOON. (*Surprised.*) What do you want?

GRISHA. Nothing. I was just . . . just looking, that's all.

CHERKOON. Who are you?

GRISHA. Grisha Redozubov. The mayor's my father. We're neighbors.

ANNA. I love the way he smiles. Invite him over, Yegor.

CHERKOON. Well, come on over. Let's get acquainted.

GRISHA. I can't climb over. I'm too fat.

ANNA. (*Laughing.*) Why don't you just come through the gate.

GRISHA. You mean out into the street and . . . and back in again?

ANNA. Yes.

GRISHA. O.K. (GRISHA *vanishes. Enter* TSYGANOV.)

ANNA. He's hilarious.

CHERKOON. So, now you'll have some entertainment.

TSYGANOV. I tried to have a nap but I couldn't sleep, damnit. The flies here, they're incredible . . . buzz buzz, smashing into the windows, bang, splat, landing on your nose, crawling into you ear . . .

CHERKOON. Not to mention the hangover after last night's festivities.

TSYGANOV. Ah, yes, they certainly do welcome you with a vengeance in these parts. What the hell was that drink they served?

CHERKOON. Pritikin called it Elephant Poison.

TSYGANOV. Well named. You know, George, I think it might have eaten away some of my brain cells. All day long I've found myself thinking about that little brunette, what was her name, chorus girl at the operetta . . . drowned herself in the Moika. Did you ever meet her?

CHERKOON. No.

TSYGANOV. (*Thoughtfully.*) Petite, lovely eyes . . . just now when I was executing this particularly persistant fly, de-winging it with my cigarette tip, I was suddenly reminded of her. What *was* her name. (ANNA *looks towards the house, starts.*)

ANNA. What on earth is that? Oh god no, look . . .

TSYGANOV. I must be hallucinating. (GRISHA *enters wearing a heavy fur coat.*)

GRISHA. Made it. Whew, it's hot.

CHERKOON. You damn fool, what's that for?

GRISHA. What? Oh, the coat. I'm called for the army this fall. I wear this coat, it'll steam all the fat off me and I'll be so thin and weak they won't want me. It's my father's idea.

TSYGANOV. Brilliant.

CHERKOON. And you let him make a complete fool out of you.

GRISHA. What can I do? He has a temper, you should see it, just like that . . . (*Snaps fingers.*) He'd bust my head open. Anyway, maybe I will get real thin and the army really won't take me.

CHERKOON. For god sake take off the coat, you look hideous. Aren't you ashamed of yourself? Every girl in town must be laughing at you. You tell your father from now on you're not going to wear a fur coat in this heat wave.

GRISHA. Tell him?! Me?! You tell him. I'd like to see that.

TSYGANOV. Now listen, my young grizzly bear, what if your father told you to get down on all fours and ordered you to carry him to town like a pony. Would you do it?

GRISHA. Oh, he'd never make me do that. He's too proud. He doesn't like people to laugh at him.

CHERKOON. Just take off the coat.

GRISHA. (*Doing so.*) Well. All right. Just for a minute. But if he catches me . . .

ANNA. You must be extremely fond of him.

GRISHA. (*Pause.*) He's old. He'll be dead soon. After that I won't have anyone over me.

CHERKOON. Go home and tell him I want to see him immediately.

GRISHA. Who? My father? Did you say *tell* him?

CHERKOON. That's right. He's at home, isn't he?

GRISHA. (*Lost.*) Yes but . . . I mean . . . how can I . . . Tell my father? He's the head of the town. (CHERKOON *jumps up and goes to the fence.*)

CHERKOON. Oh for god sake . . .

GRISHA. What are you doing. Ma'am, what's he up to? I'm getting out of here. You're all crazy.

CHERKOON. (*Shouts over the fence.*) Hey, anybody home? Hey, Mr. Mayor . . . Come over here, I want a word with you.

ANNA. (*Laughing.*) Yegor, stop it, you're going too far.

GRISHA. He is, ma'am. I'm going to be in such hot water. It's not fair, I didn't want to come over, you made me . . .

REDOZUBOV. (*Behind fence.*) Grisha . . . Grisha . . . !

GRISHA. Oh god, oh god, he's looking for me.

CHERKOON. (*Over fence.*) He's over here with us.

TSYGANOV. (*Seeing* PELAGAYA.) Look . . . another specimen of the local wildlife.

GRISHA. Oh no, it's Pelagaya Pritikina . . . now I've had it . . .

TSYGANOV. I think I know what you need, my boy. A good, stiff drink.

GRISHA. Oh please, please yes, anything . . . quick.

ANNA. (*Laughing.*) Oh come on, now, it's not that bad . . . Styopa!

PELAGEYA. Good morning.

TSYGANOV. And to what do we owe the honor?

PELAGEYA. Is Tatiana Nikolayevna at home?

TSYGANOV. Ah, dear lady, that's the one question I can't answer. (*Enter* STYOPA.)

PELAGEYA. Ah, Grisha, good morning.

GRISHA. (*Muttering.*) Here it comes.

CHERKOON. What's this? You're being greeted by a lady and you don't stand up?

ANNA. (*To* STYOPA.) Bring us the port and some liqueurs. (*As* STYOPA *goes in* TSYGANOV *calls after her.*)

TSYGANOV. And brandy, and vodka.

GRISHA. But I know her.

PELAGEYA. Of course he does, we know each other. And this beautiful lady must be your wife.

CHERKOON. And she doesn't know where Tatiana Nikolayevna is either. (STYOPA *returns with trayful of bottles, glasses.*)

PELAGEYA. Oh, that's all right. I'll tell you a little secret. I didn't really come to see her. I can see her any time I want to, but it's a great honor to be meeting you.

CHERKOON. She must mean you, Anna.

TSYGANOV. (*To* ANNA.) Must be. Well, my boy, what's your pleasure?

GRISHA. Something with a kick to it.

PELAGEYA. No, I mean everybody. Your wife, too, of course, it's always exciting to see the lastest fashions in dress, but you, too, the two of you are also both very interesting, really.

GRISHA. (*Drinking.*) Yeech, it's sweet. But I like it.

TSYGANOV. (*Bows to* PELAGAYA.) Most honored, madame. (*To* GRISHA.) The name of that beverage . . . burn it on your mind, my boy . . . it's called chartreuse.

ANNA. (*To* PELAGAYA.) Please, sit down.

PELAGEYA. Merci. You know, I keep saying to Arkhip, that's my husband, I said 'You awful thing, you, why don't you introduce me to those engineers' and he tries to frighten me. They're too snooty for you, he says, but I don't think you're snooty at all, I knew you wouldn't be. Of course you're educated so you're proud but why shouldn't you be proud, everybody has to be proud of something. We're proud of our money, you're proud of your education. Anyone who doesn't have something to be proud of is like a . . . what's he like . . . like a baby that only lived a year and then died so there's nothing you can say about him. I know because I gave birth to a child like that once. . . .

ANNA. (*Rising quickly.*) Why don't you walk to the veranda with me.

PELAGEYA. With pleasure, my dear. You're such a lovely woman, so warmhearted. We've very glad you're here, very glad. Isn't our little town a charming place, we have woods, meadows, swamps, blueberries. Oh, the blueberries are so abundant and plentiful, we're just completely surrounded by lovely environs.

TSYGANOV. (*Looking after the ladies.*) She's very funny, isn't she, Georges. A real original.

GRISHA. (*Laughs.*) She's dumb.

CHERKOON. What?

GRISHA. She's dumb. Old woman like that goes and marries a young man. She had money. He took it all.

And he plays around, too. He's no fool, her husband.
REDOZUBOV. Grisha!
GRISHA. Oh lord, my father's coming. Where can I hide? I better have another drink. (TSYGANOV *stands in front of* GRISHA *who pours himself a large glass of liqueur, knocks it back, rolls his eyes wildly. Enter* REDOZUBOV, *looking furtively at* CHERKOON. *He is followed by* PAVLIN, *who carries a large exercise book.*)
REDOZUBOV. (*Not bowing.*) Grishka. Who said you could come here?
GRISHA. Err . . . no one.
CHERKOON. I invited him.
REDOZUBOV. What for?
CHERKOON. I felt like it.
REDOZUBOV. Did you ask him if he'd gotten my permission?
CHERKOON. No. Why should I? (*They watch each other in silence.*)
REDOZUBOV. I'm his father.
CHERKOON. Well, I haven't got time for a long discussion right now. I don't want to see your son wearing that idiotic coat any more. It's ridiculous.
REDOZUBOV. (*Amazed.*) What? What???!!! (PAVLIN *walks cautiously away from* REDOZUBOV.)
CHERKOON. You heard me. If I see that coat on him one more time I'll write to the military authorities and tell them you're forcing your son to evade military service. Is that clear, Mr. Mayor?
GRISHA. (*Blurts out.*) Papa, I want to go in the army, I swear I do.
REDOZUBOV. (*Lost.*) Quiet. What gives you the right . . .
GRISHA. I can't get any thinner, papa, I just can't. . . . (PRITIKIN *appears on the* L. *and stands behind trees.*)
REDOZUBOV. (*More calmly.*) Grisha, go home! You

came here to build the railway, mister. All right, build it. I don't interfere with your business, you keep out of mine. (*To* GRISHA.) And you, put your eyes back in your head and get home. (*To* CHERKOON.) You'll hear about this, believe me. I'll be speaking to the governor.

TSYGANOV. (*Gentle smile.*) You'll be doing your speaking in front of a judge. That won't be very nice now, will it? A sixty year old man, mayor of the town, churchwarden, godfather to the son of the Chief of the Fire Brigade, etcetera, etcetera, such a brilliant career and such a shameful end. . . .

REDOZUBOV. Grisha, go home. Don't listen to them. Cover your ears. Don't even look at them.

GRISHA. (*Drunk, weeping.*) They'll send you to prison. They'll send me to prison. They'll send us both to prison. (REDOZUBOV *grabs* GRISHA *by the hand.*)

REDOZUBOV. Come on, you stupid mutt. (*They exit quickly, pursued by* CHERKOON.)

CHERKOON. (*Calm.*) And if you lay a hand on that boy you'll pay for it. (CHERKOON *follows them off.*)

PRITYKIN. (*Amazed.*) He was scared. Vassily Redozubov, scared . . .

TSYGANOV. He likes everyone to bow and scrape, doesn't he.

PRITYKIN. Oh, yes, he's a fanatic about it. At a funeral, if he saw a dead man getting respect he'd want to jump in the coffin and take his place. You know those two huge pillars in front of his house? He swore he was going to have a front porch as big as a castle even if it meant blocking the whole street. They told him he wasn't allowed but he went right ahead anyway so they had to take him to court. The case has been going on for six years. He knows he can't win but he won't give in to anything. (PAVLIN *steps forward, counting off the charges on his fingers.*)

PAVLIN. And permit me to add that he's a very cruel man. He beat one wife into the grave, the other ran off to a convent, one of his sons is a simpleton and the other one disappeared without a trace.

TSYGANOV. And permit *me* to ask who are you?

PAVLIN. Me? I'm known to everyone here.

PRITYKIN. He's a friend of Redozubov . . . and a treacherous snake in the grass.

PAVLIN. I stive to be on friendly terms with all reasonable men.

TSYGANOV. Did you want something?

PAVLIN. Indeed I did, sir. (*Holds out notebook.*) I have here a work written by myself. You're an educated man, I'd like your opinion of it. I've entitled it "An Essay of the Implication of Certain Words Written by a Disinterested Lover of the Truth in Order to Expose Lies and Falsehood." It's the humble labor of nine years.

TSYGANOV. Yes, the title alone, I should think. (*Takes book.*) And what is the thrust of your augument?

PAVLIN. I'm against new words. Men have acted the same way since time immemorial, but we constantly obscure the issue by giving their actions new names. This is what I object to. In a general sense I stand firmly against new words.

TSYGANOV. Give me an example.

PAVLIN. For instance, take the word slanderer. This was always an adequate word, but recently it's been changed to 'newspaper reporter.'

TSYGANOV. You've lost me.

PRITYKIN. He's talking about the local newspaper. When our schoolmaster killed himself they found out Pavlin had denounced him to the authorities and they published an expose. I bet you wouldn't denounce Mayor Redozubov for anything *he* did. . . .

PAVLIN. Arkhip Fomich, how could I do that? I am a humble bush. The Mayor is a towering oak. He is above, I am below. This is as it should be.

TSYGANOV. All right, I'll have a look at your manuscript.

PAVLIN. I am grateful beyond words.

TSYGANOV. Drop by some time.

PAVLIN. I'll make it my duty to do so. (*All three exit. Above* REDOZUBOV's *fence appears the head of* KATYA, *the mayor's daughter. She looks around the deserted garden.* CHERKOON's *voice is heard,* KATYA *vanishes. Enter* CHERKOON *and* ANNA.)

ANNA. You shouldn't make fun of people like that just because they're ignorant.

CHERKOON. They're beasts.

ANNA. Only because they're ignorant.

CHERKOON. God, you're predictable.

ANNA. Why do you have to make everything so difficult, Yegor?

CHERKOON. You find things difficult? Funny, I just find them boring. (*He sits at the table.*) Your guests are waiting for you.

ANNA. I know. I'm going. Don't you want to kiss me?

CHERKOON. No. (ANNA *turns quickly and goes out.* CHERKOON *works.* KATYA *appears again over the fence, throws a stone at* CHERKOON, *then a stick. She vanishes.*)

CHERKOON. (*Towards fence.*) Hey, what are you doing? Savages. Stop it. I'm warning you.

KATYA. You don't scare me.

CHERKOON. (*Standing.*) You a woman?

KATYA. None of your business.

CHERKOON. Well, whatever you are, you shouldn't throw stones at people, you could hurt someone like that.

KATYA. Look who's talking. You hurt people.
CHERKOON. What people?
KATYA. Ha, what people! That's a good one. My father. My brother.
CHERKOON. Ah, so that's it. Still, you shouldn't attack from behind a fence. Come out and show yourself. (*Enter* STEPAN, *who looks at* CHERKOON *with surprise.*)
KATYA. I'm not afraid of you.
CHERKOON. I'm sure you're not. But I'll bet you're ugly. That's why you don't want me to see you, isn't it?
STEPAN. Who are you talking to, chief?
CHERKOON. A lady.
STEPAN. Where is she?
CHERKOON. Behind there.
STEPAN. What's going on? The Chief of Police wants to see you.
CHERKOON. What for?
STEPAN. Don't know. I think I'll have a look at this lady.
KATYA. Don't you dare.
CHERKOON. (*Exiting.*) Careful. She throws stones at men who get too close.
KATYA. Only at redheads.
STEPAN. You're not going to hit me with that stick, are you?
KATYA. Come a little closer, you'll find out.
STEPAN. Hmmm. I'm scared. Still, maybe it's worth the risk. . . . (KATYA *appears at the fence suddenly.*)
KATYA. No, stay back. If my father sees you there'll be hell to pay. What do you want?
STEPAN. Nothing. What do *you* want?
KATYA. When that redhead comes back I'm going to smash his nose with a rock.
STEPAN. My, my, what's he done to you?

KATYA. None of your business. Is that woman his wife? The beautiful one?

STEPAN. Why do you want to know?

KATYA. Because I do. Does he love her?

STEPAN. You'll have to ask him. Or her.

KATYA. I'm asking you.

STEPAN. I'm afraid I'm not an expert on that subject.

KATYA. Yes you are. Students know all about things like that. They're degenerate. They don't believe in God and they read books that aren't allowed . . . forbidden books . . . I know all about students. Do you read books . . . like that?

STEPAN. Alas, I do. Horrifying, isn't it? (*Enter* TSYGANOV. *He listens, smiling.*)

KATYA. Shame on you. Why do you do it?

STEPAN. Because I'm a student. We're all degenerate.

KATYA. Do you have one you could lend me? A really good one, though. I like to read. Would you. Oh! (*Seeing* TSYGANOV, *she disappears.* STEPAN *looks and sees* TSYGANOV.)

TSYGANOV. Congratulations.

STEPAN. (*Embarrassed.*) What do you mean? Oh, that; that was nothing. She wants to borrow some books, that's all. Talked across the fence. Look, it's nothing.

TSYGANOV. I haven't said a word.

STEPAN. No, but you're smiling. I know what you're thinking.

TSYGANOV. Well, you're still making sense, so I guess it isn't love quite yet.

STEPAN. Don't be silly. There's no such thing as love.

TSYGANOV. Ah, yes, many's the time I've told myself exactly that, but it never helped, I still fell in love. She's pretty, isn't she? Fuzzy little spitfire. Good luck. (TSYGANOV *goes out, taking a bundle of maps from the table.* STEPAN *looks over the fence, then makes a move to climb it. Enter* BOGAYEVSKAYA *and* NADIEZHDA.)

BOGAYEVSKAYA. I see our little town's making you climb the walls already.

STEPAN. My cap. I hung it on the fence . . . it fell down the other side.

BOGAYEVSKAYA. And bounced back up onto your head again.

STEPAN. Not this cap . . . a different one. I have several.

BOGAYEVSKAYA. I think it's your head you lost, not your cap. Nadiezhda Polikarpovna let me introduce Stepan Danilovich Lukin. (NADIEZHDA *looks intently at him.*)

NADIEZHDA. Just a baby.

BOGAYEVSKAYA. So we'll leave him to play climb-the-fence, shall we? By the way, Nadiezhda, you'd appear a great deal smarter if you didn't talk so much. (STYOPA *enters with a basket of crockery, bottles of lemonade, liqueurs. She collects the papers on the table, spreads a cloth. The* DOCTOR, TSYGANOV *and* ANNA *appear.*)

NADIEZHDA. (*Calmly.*) I have a very good mind.

BOGAYEVSKAYA. Nonsense. Apart from all that babbling about love there's not a single other subject you can talk about, do you realise that?

NADIEZHDA. Yes, I talk only about love.

TSYGANOV. (*To* DOCTOR.) To start with, a drink, what do you say, doctor.

DR. MAKAROV. And to continue with, another drink.

TSYGANOV. What else? Is everything here, Styopa? Now, what have we here . . . ? (TSYGANOV *busies himself with the bottles. The* DOCTOR *stares at*

BARBARIANS   51

NADIEZHDA *with a somber, steady gaze.* ANNA *enters and sits next to her.)*

ANNA. You must get very bored, living here.

NADIEZHDA. Some people find it boring. I don't. There's always books to read, or one can just sit and think.

ANNA. What kind of books. Novels?

NADIEZHDA. What else is there? We used to have a man here, a statistician, but he shot himself in the end. . . .

ANNA. Shot himself? Why did he do that?

DR. MAKAROV. (*Darkly and angrily.*) Because he loved her . . .

BOGAYEVSKAYA. Doctor, please . . .

NADIEZHDA. He used to give me other kinds of books to read . . . not romances . . . but they were so boring.

TSYGANOV. What about in the town? Do you have real true live romances here?

NADIEZHDA. Of course. Love happens everywhere, even here.

ANNA. Love among the locals. It must be terribly sad.

NADIEZHDA. Why? Love is the same wherever it happens . . . if it's true love.

TSYGANOV. What is true love, tell me.

NADIEZHDA. The kind that never changes. The kind that never dies.

TSYGANOV. Yes, you have read a lot, haven't you? And I suppose you've had more than your share of men fall in love with you.

NADIEZHDA. Not expecially. The man that shot himself, he used to write me long letters, and before him there was a council chairman he used to talk to me about love all the time but then he'd go off hunting. He caught a cold when he went out in the woods

drunk. He died three days later. (*The* DOCTOR *walks slowly away.* ANNA *shudders.*)
ANNA. He died.
NADIEZHDA. Yes, but I didn't really like him. He drank alot and made wheezing noises all the time and had a red face. Now it's the doctor here, he says he's in love with me. . . .
BOGAYEVSKAYA. My dear, I wish you'd learn to keep quiet, really . . . (BOGAYEVSKAYA *gets up and goes into the house. The* DOCTOR *is standing under the trees, gazing at* NADIEZHDA, *motionless.*)
ANNA. (*Crushed.*) You talk about these things . . . so calmly.
TSYGANOV. And what do you feel towards him?
NADIEZHDA. The doctor? Nothing. He's the same as my husband.
TSYGANOV. I don't find them a bit alike.
NADIEZHDA. But they are. Not the way they look, but underneath, their souls are identical. They even both like to fish, and anyone who likes fishing is already halfway to the grave, just sitting for hours hunched over the water waiting for death to come.
TSYGANOV. (*To* ANNA.) She has a point there.
ANNA. Yegor would enjoy that.
NADIEZHDA. Oh, your husband. He has such fascinating eyes. And his hair, it's like fire. He's really a striking person . . . once seen, never forgotten. All the men here have the same kind of eyes . . . in fact, they have no eyes at all.
ANNA. (*Softly.*) You're a very strange woman.
TSYGANOV. Yes, even a bit frightening.
NADIEZHDA. (*Smiling for the first time.*) Do you really think so?
TSYGANOV. With all my heart.

NADIEZHDA. That's interesting. The doctor said the same thing to me.

ANNA. (*Quietly.*) Poor man. (MONAKHOV's *voice can be heard. He is laughing. Enter* CHERKOON, THE CHIEF OF POLICE [YAKOV ALERKSEYICH], MONOKHOV, LYDIA *and* BOGAYEVSKAYA.)

CHERKOON. Anna! The Chief of Police is leaving. (*He remains to one side with* LYDIA.)

ANNA. Won't you stay with us a little longer. Please, sit down.

CHIEF OF POLICE. You're too kind, madam, but I think that's enough for the first visit. You know what, Sergei Nikolayich, I seem to have gone right through your sherry. Didn't even notice. Very fine, very fine.

TSYGANOV. (*Vacantly.*) We'll be getting more of the same, very soon.

CHIEF OF POLICE. You know where to find me. (CHIEF OF POLICE *laughs loudly.* MONAHKOV *approaches the* DOCTOR.)

MONAKHOV. So, my friend, how goes it?

DR. MAKAROV. Fine. I need some more beer.

MONAKHOV. Why not. Drown your sorrows, eh?

CHIEF OF POLICE. So, what's tomorrow, an outing on the river, isn't it? I'll send over some horses from the Fire Brigade at five o'clock sharp. And what would you say to a little music?

BOGAYEVSKAYA. Please god, spare us that, we'd all be deaf by sunset. Besides, what if there's a fire, the men will be needed in town.

CHIEF OF POLICE. Perish the thought. I hate fires. Whenever there's a fire we're all in hot water. (*Laughs loudly.*) Well, I'm gone. Farewell, good-bye and au revoir. Wonderful to have folks like you in our town ... well, enough of that. I'm no good at speechifying. ...

NADIEZHDA. Did you bring your carriage?

CHIEF OF POLICE. Does the sun bring light? Would you like a lift home? Honor me, fair maiden.

TSYGANOV. Do you have to go so soon, Nadiezhda? Stay for a while.

NADIEZHDA. No, I should be going. Good-bye, Mavriky. Good-bye Anna Fyodorovna, I'm going home now.

MONAKHOV. Home. Ah, good, Nadya, that's wonderful.

ANNA. I'll always be delighted to see you.

TSYGANOV. And so shall I.

CHIEF OF POLICE. Yes, she's a very nice thing to see, no doubt about it. Your arm, ma'am! Anna Fyodorovna, all good things to you. Sergei Nikolayich . . . I look forward to certain liquid arrivals and Tatiana Bogayevskaya . . . I wish you pleasant dreams.

BOGAYEVSKAYA. Isn't it a little early in the day for that? But it's the thought that counts, I suppose.

CHIEF OF POLICE. Nothing is too good for you, dear madam. You know, I'll have to remember to thank the Mayor for this. He's a persnickety little pain in the you know where, but if he hadn't made a complaint, I might have never had the pleasure of your acquaintance. Blessings on you, one and all. (*He exits with* NADIEZHDA *on his arm.* ANNA *goes up to the* DOCTOR.)

ANNA. Doctor, would you like to take a little stroll in the garden?

DR. MAKAROV. All right. Let's go.

ANNA. You could at least say, "I'd be delighted".

DR. MAKAROV. Forgive me. I've forgotten how to speak the human language. (*They exit, talking.* CHERKOON *and* LYDIA, *talking quietly, both serious, apporach the table.* TSYGANOV *gazes after* NADIEZHDA, *pours himself a large glass of something and drinks.* MONAHKOV, *standing by the table, smacks his lips in approval.*)

CHERKOON. Careful, Sergei, you're drinking yourself to death.

TSYGANOV. And you, Georges, you should learn better manners. Why don't you enroll for some lessons with the Chief of Police?

CHERKOON. (*To* LYDIA.) Lydia, one moment. (*To* TSYGANOV.) Sergei, listen, that awful woman, the tax collector's wife, she keeps staring at me with those greedy eyes.

TSYGANOV. You're an idiot, Georges. Which, as it turns out, is very lucky for me. I think you're being waited for. (CHERKOON *shrugs and returns to* LYDIA.) Mavriky Osipovich . . . how about a drink?

MONAKHOV. Even on death's doorstep I wouldn't say no.

TSYGANOV. A man after my own heart. Cigar? You don't happen to play cards, do you?

MONAKHOV. For what other reason did God give us hands?

TSYGANOV. Ah, and a sense of humor, too. A beautiful wife, a rapier wit . . . what else . . . ?

MONAKHOV. (*Interrupting.*) Would you like to make a bet?

TSYGANOV. A bet? On what?

MONAKHOV. I'll bet a hundred roubles to your fifty that you fall in love with my wife. What do you say?

TSYGANOV. (*Regards him haughtily.*) You have no objections? (MONAHKOV *draws a zero in the air with his finger.*)

MONAKHOV. Zero. You have my blessings.

TSYGANOV. (*More emphatically.*) And if . . . just

speaking theoretically, of course . . . what happens if she falls in love with me?

MONAKHOV. Five hundred says she won't. To your one hundred if she does.

TSYGANOV. (*Laughs.*) You're a funny man, you know that? I'll tell you what. I think I'll pass for now. Let's have a game of cards instead. Get the Doctor. And Pritikin's inside checking the accounts with our student. I wonder how long before he'll find a way to cheat us. (*They go towards the house. Indoors we hear* ANNA *playing a sad tune on the piano.*)

MONAKHOV. Not long.

TSYGANOV. It's odd the way everyone seems to be shrinking. Only the crooks get bigger and bigger. (MONAHKOV *laughs loudly.* CHERKOON *and* LYDIA *appear from among the trees. They walk slowly, stop beside the table and continue to talk without sitting down.*)

CHERKOON. Will you be staying here for long?

LYDIA. I don't know. Probably a month or so.

CHERKOON. I'm stuck here till winter it looks like . . . late fall at least.

LYDIA. I don't like small towns. They make everything seem insignificant. You look at them and you think "What's the point?"

CHERKOON. I know. Energy just seems to stop dead here. Frozen. In the big cities things are always humming . . . you can feel it day and night, the excitement, the struggle, the fight for life. Lights burning, music playing. Everything the world has to offer.

LYDIA. I think of it as a kind of symphony . . . like an enchanted castle where you can find everything and it's yours for the asking. It makes you want to live, a big city.

CHERKOON. To live, yes, exactly, to live, that's what I

want. I'm greedy for life. Everything that's bad in this world; I've seen it. Everything harsh and ugly; I've known it. There was a time, you know, when people made me feel worthless just because I was hungry. Do you know how humiliating it is when a man has to live from day to day knowing his clothes are filthy and his fingernails uncut. . . .

LYDIA. You can't get those times out of your mind, can you. . . .

CHERKOON. Never. All I want is to get even with the people who stepped on me and tried to keep me back. It's essential. Every ounce of pity's been burned out of me, all the indulgence for those grasping, stupid animals in power, the ones who rule our lives . . . and the feeble minded fools who let themselves be humiliated and abused. It makes me murderous just to think about it.

LYDIA. Even now life isn't easy for you, is it?

CHERKOON. Now? No, not even now.

LYDIA. (*Makes a wide circle with her hand.*) This is no place for you to be. What you need is a wide battlefield to command . . . you seem capable of something extraordinary . . . something significant . . . you're so direct, so driven. But you don't seem to know your own worth. You know, it's not a sin to overvalue yourself a little, give yourself an impossible goal to reach for. But to sell yourself for too small a price . . . it's just kneeling down to let other people jump over you.

CHERKOON. I'm aware of all that.

LYDIA. It seems to me a man needs very little, but what he has should be truly excellent. We always seem to clutter up our lives with trivial things . . . the second rate. The only way our lives will ever be beautiful is when people stand up and demand what's rare and excellent.

CHERKOON. You're a romantic.

LYDIA. Is that such a bad thing to be? Isn't that what we should aim for? Someone's coming. (*Enter* DUNYA'S HUSBAND. *He is more tattered than in Act I . . . Drunk, swaggering slightly.*)

CHERKOON. What do you want?

DUNYA'S HUSBAND. (*With inspiration.*) I have news for you, sir. I'm the father.

CHERKOON. Whose father?

DUNYA'S HUSBAND. Hers. Your maid. Stepinida. My daughter. She's a runaway. She ran away from me so . . . so she's a runaway. And therefore I demand. I'm her father. I have a right.

CHERKOON. (*To* LYDIA.) That's what my father was like.

LYDIA. Tell him to go away. He's disgusting.

CHERKOON. What are you demanding?

DUNYA'S HUSBAND. Her wages. Whose daughter is she? Mine. So her wages are mine, too. Therefore . . . I demand them. Otherwise, I'll take her back. My daughter. Pavlin says no one can keep someone else's daughter if she's a runaway. And the father can demand the wages. Always. Pavlin says so. Always.

CHERKOON. You're no father. You think siring someone gives you the right to call yourself a father. Any animal can do that. A father's a man. You're not even that.

LYDIA. (*Laughing.*) You're so naive. Do you expect him to follow that kind of thinking?

CHERKOON. No, of course not. Go on, get out of here.

DUNYA'S HUSBAND. (*Retreating.*) What about Stepinida's wages.

CHERKOON. Go away . . . go!

DUNYA'S HUSBAND. (*Scared, sobering slightly.*) I'm

going . . . I'm going . . . at least you could let me have fifty copeks . . .

LYDIA. (*Throws coin.*) There, now leave us alone.

CHERKOON. Get out. (DUNYA'S HUSBAND *exits without looking around.* ANNA *looks on, half-hidden by the bushes.*)

LYDIA. (*Smiling.*) It's incredible. He just trades his own daughter for a miserable piece of metal. And we're supposed to feel compassion for these people, love them even, can you believe that? Sympathy won't do them any good, and how can you love them? Ah, here comes Anna Fyodrovna. Have the guests tired you already?

ANNA. (*Coldly.*) I'm fine, thank you. They're playing cards. I just came out for a look.

CHERKOON. (*Suspiciously.*) A look at what?

ANNA. I saw that pathetic creature coming into the garden.

LYDIA. Well, I think I'll be going home. I'll be seeing you this evening so I won't say good-bye.

CHERKOON. Yes . . . till tonight. (*Exit* LYDIA. CHERKOON *looks after her.* ANNA *watches him, biting her lip.* STYOPA *rushes in to her.*)

STYOPA. Did he come for me? Did he want me?

ANNA. No, Styopa. He just . . . came by, that's all. There's nothing to worry about.

STYOPA. Don't give me back to him, please, I beg you. . . .

ANNA. You know we wouldn't do that, now stop torturing yourself.

STYOPA. I'll go to the convent. I will. They wouldn't let him into the convent, would they? I'd be safe there.

CHERKOON. Don't be ridiculous, Styopa, there's nothing he can do to you. Now run along.

ANNA. We won't let him take you away from us . . . we promise.

STYOPA. (*Exiting.*) Oh lord, oh lord . . .

ANNA. Yegor, we have to do something to make that man understand.

CHERKOON. (*Brusquely.*) We'll do nothing at all.

ANNA. (*Gently.*) Are you angry?

CHERKOON. No. But you could be less obvious about the fact that you don't like Lydia Pavlovna.

ANNA. Now wait a minute, Yegor, what did I do to make you think I don't like her?

CHERKOON. Anna, what's the point of lying to me? We know each other too well. I like her. I find her interesting. You sense that and you're frightened.

ANNA. (*Anxious.*) Frightened? Why should I be afraid? I'm not at all . . . I'm not.

CHERKOON. It's obvious, Anna . . .

ANNA. What? What do you mean? Tell me, just say it . . . no, no don't. Don't say anything.

CHERKOON. (*Fiercely.*) Anna, calm down . . .

ANNA. Don't say anything. Just let me get used to the idea. . . .

CHERKOON. The idea's been in your head for a long time. Aren't you used to it yet?

ANNA. I can't accept it, I'm sorry, I can't. I love you, Yegor, you know that, I love you. Whatever you do I'll forgive you.

CHERKOON. I don't need your forgiveness.

ANNA. I know I'm ordinary, I know that, I'm not an interesting person, but I love you and I can't help it but I need you. You can't hate me for that, can you? I know you're not that cruel.

CHERKOON. I don't hate you, that's not true. But I don't love you any more. That is truth.

ANNA. But you did once. No, wait, I don't believe it, it can't be true.

CHERKOON. I feel nothing. I'm sorry, I can't pretend. Only lechers and cheats stay with their wives when they don't love them any more.

ANNA. No, no, wait, please. Give me some time. I'll try . . . I can be different . . . I'll make myself more interesting for you.

CHERKOON. Anna, don't talk like that. How can you demean yourself, don't you have any pride, for god sake.

ANNA. But I . . . oh darling . . . I can't live without you.

CHERKOON. (*Firmly.*) And I can't live *with* you. (*He goes inside.* ANNA, *crushed, sits slowly at the table. A noise, someone is heard climbing over the fence.* ANNA *doesn't hear.* KATYA *comes running out from under the tree, rushes to* ANNA *and hugs her.*)

KATYA. Don't cry, please, you're so lovely and gentle and he's such a horrible man, he's a pig. . . .

ANNA. (*Jumps up.*) Get away. Who are you?

KATYA. And he's a fool. How can he talk to you like that? How could anyone not love you?

ANNA. Who are you? How did you . . .

KATYA. I'm Katya . . . Katya Redozubov, the mayor's daughter. Get rid of him, leave him . . . you're still young and beautiful, you'll find someone to love, someone good and kind. You just leave him to me, I'll beat his brains out.

ANNA. Oh my god, were you listening . . . ?

KATYA. I know everything that goes on over here. I've been watching you people all day long through the cracks in the fence and I love you so much.

ANNA. (*Regaining composure slightly.*) You know

it's not very nice to spy on people.

KATYA. Why not? We're supposed to learn everything we can in life, and it's been really interesting. And anyway, if I hadn't seen you I wouldn't have come over and then you'd be sitting here crying all by yourself and this way I'm here to keep you company. (*Enter* STEPAN.)

ANNA. (*To* KATYA.) Don't say anything about this to anyone. Do you understand? Nothing happened. You didn't hear anything. Promise me.

KATYA. (*Importantly.*) My lips are sealed. Oh no, it's him! (STEPAN *takes off cap and bows.*)

STEPAN. It is I, in person. May I ask if you did us the honor of scaling the fence. . . .

KATYA. None of your business. You think if I climbed over I'm not so smart but I'm as smart as you are any day. Kindly leave us now.

STEPAN. What did I do to deserve such wrath?

KATYA. (*Stamps foot.*) Be quiet! You don't even know how to talk to people. (*To* ANNA, *taking her arm.*) Let's go.

ANNA. I'm sorry, I can't . . . I haven't really got time . . .

KATYA. I understand. I'll just keep you company. Come with me. (*She takes* ANNA *towards the end of the garden. Enter* REDOZUBOV *and* PAVLIN. REDOZUBOV *is dishevelled and excited.*)

REDOZUBOV. Pavlin, you're a witness. They lured my son over here, they made him drunk. Now they've taken my daughter. (*To* STEPAN.) Who are you? Are you with the engineers? Tell them the Mayor's here to see them. Now, Pavlin, watch this.

STEPAN. I think you've made a mistake, sir.

PAVLIN. The young man is actually a student, not a . . .

REDOZUBOV. Aha, there you are. Birds of a feather. They're anacrists, that's what they are. Go on, get them out here.

STEPAN. Why should I?

REDOZUBOV. Whaaaat?!! I'm telling you . . . I'm ordering you . . . (*Enter* CHERKOON.)

CHERKOON. What seems to be the trouble?

REDOZUBOV. Where's my daughter?

CHERKOON. How should I know?

REDOZUBOV. You're lying. (*To* PAVLIN.) You see, that's anacrism, pure and simple.

CHERKOON. What's anacrism?

STEPAN. Never heard of it.

REDOZUBOV. This is not a joke. I want my daughter.

PAVLIN. You might think he means anarchism, but he's actually saying antichristian and using the technically correct pronunciation.

CHERKOON. Listen, old man, your daughter was here a while ago throwing rocks at my head and I'm afraid that's the last I saw of her, all right? (KATYA *runs in.*)

REDOZUBOV. And who is this? Katya, who gave you permission . . . ?

KATYA. Now don't get excited. Come to me . . . come on, don't be afraid of him, he's not going to touch you.

REDOZUBOV. This is no place for you to be spending time.

KATYA. (*To* CHERKOON.) And don't you say a word . . . yes, you know who I'm talking to . . . pig. (*She exits, leading her father off.* STEPAN *laughs.* CHERKOON *smiles at him.* PAVLIN *looks on, thin lipped.*)

CHERKOON. It's amazing, she flounces in, takes over, starts ordering people around . . . huh.

STEPAN. (*Laughs.*) She's really something, isn't she?

CHERKOON. I suppose I ought to have a word with the old man. (GRISHA'S *head appears over the fence. He looks around.*)

PAVLIN. Permit me to say that you've upset him considerably, sir.

CHERKOON. (*To* STEPAN.) Who's this?

STEPAN. The conscience of the king, and the local weathervane . . . changes with the wind.

GRISHA. Hey, mister.

CHERKOON. Yes?

GRISHA. He didn't hit me. I swear . . . not a smack . . . (KATYA *runs in.*)

KATYA. Hey you. My father wants you. Come on. What are you smiling at? I know all about you . . . Red! (*Laughs. She sticks out her tongue and runs off.* STEPAN *brusts out laughing.* PAVLIN *doen't know how to react.* CHERKOON *smiles and follows* KATYA *out.* GRISHA *watches apprehensively.*)

CURTAIN

ACT THREE

Two months later.

The same garden. The sun is setting. Colored lights hanging in the trees. Wine and snacks are set out on the table. MATVEY, *dressed very neatly now, is opening beer bottles under the trees.* PRITIKIN *stands at the end of the garden. Beside him* MONAKHOV *plays softly on the clarinet.*

Noise and bustle coming from inside the house. Someone is at the piano playing 'Siskin' with one finger and keeps getting it wrong. The CHIEF OF POLICE *can be heard laughing loudly.* STYOPA *is busy arranging things on the table.*

MATVEY. Know how much I've saved up already? Almost three hundred roubles.

STYOPA. So what?

MATVEY. Proves I'm not stupid.

STYOPA. I never said you were. But you're greedy, that's for sure, just like all the other peasants, all you ever talk about is money.

MATVEY. I'm not a peasant. (CHERKOON *enters and moves over to the table, followed by* NADIEZHDA.)

CHERKOON. Styopa, give me a little Seltzer. (*To* NAD.) So, you had to get some fresh air too, eh? It's stuffy in there, isn't it?

NADIEZHDA. Oh . . . it's not so bad.

CHERKOON. Do you realise how strange it is, the way you look at me. Are you aware of that?

NADIEZHDA. No.

CHERKOON. (*With a laugh.*) Would you like something cold to drink. A Seltzer?

NADIEZHDA. No. I don't want anything.

CHERKOON. Well, then, I guess I'll just go in and finish the game. (CHERKOON *goes back towards the house.* NADIEZHDA *follows him slowly.*)

MATVEY. (*Obstinately.*) Anyway, what if I am a peasant, it doesn't matter. Stepan Danilich, he's a student, he knows about these things and he told me how it goes. Peasants is all there was at first, everybody was the same, and then the ones with a little brains got to be the bosses and the higher up people, that's all.

STYOPA. Don't give me that, that's stupid talk.

MATVEY. I'll give you something else when we're married. I'm strong as they come, you know, it's true, I am.

STYOPA. (*As if to herself.*) I'll go to the convent. (*Enter* CHIEF OF POLICE *and* TSYGANOV, *both drunk.*)

MATVEY. (*Laughing.*) Don't talk silly. The convent . . . that's crazy.

TSYGANOV. (*Pouring wine.*) She's an epic creature, that woman.

CHIEF OF POLICE. Yes, she's untamed, that's the problem, like an animal in the woods. I've been after her for two years, and I'm no slouch, you know, military type and all that. But, no, you're not a hero, she tells me. I'm not? Why not? Maybe I am . . . who knows. Anyway, what's a hero, tell me that? It's ridiculous. Stuck away in a little town like this and what's she looking for . . . a hero! (MONAKHOV *and* PRITIKIN *come to the table.* BOGAYEVSKAYA *shouts from the house.*)

BOGAYEVSKAYA. Yakov Alexeyich, it's your turn to deal. (*The* CHIEF OF POLICE *walks off, carrying something to eat.*)

BARBARIANS

CHIEF OF POLICE. Here I come, ready or not.

TSYGANOV. (*To* MONAKHOV.) Guess who we were talking about . . . again. Your wife.

MONAKHOV. How nice. And what were you saying about her, if it's not a state secret?

TSYGANOV. We were trying to figure out what makes her tick. So far no luck.

PAVLIN. A woman is not an easy thing to understand.

MONAKHOV. Are you talking about our little friend at the post office?

PRITYKIN. (*Tugging his sleeve.*) No, no, in general, I mean. There aren't too many men around who really understand a woman.

MONAKHOV. My friend, I understand what I need to and what I don't need to understand I don't think about.

PRITYKIN. Well, of course that's one way of looking at it . . . certainly makes for peace of mind . . . and then of course one can't expect to understand everything in the world.

TSYGANOV. How exactly did you find her?

MONAKHOV. During a service at the parish school . . . I looked, and there she was. (NADIEZHDA *is entering,* DOCTOR *with her.*)

PRITYKIN. Speak of the devil . . . look, the Doctor's with her. (*He laughs.* MONAKHOV *echoes him quietly.* TSYGANOV *looks at them contemptuously.*)

MONAKHOV. (*To* TYSGANOV.) You know, she doesn't approve of that deMaupassant fellow you gave her to read. Says it's boring and the stories are too short. I had a look, I thought he was pretty good . . . and some of the little touches . . . terrific stuff.

TSYGANOV. Nadiezhsa Polikarpovna . . . more champagne.

NADIEZHDA. Please. It's a lovely drink, all those bubbles.

MONAKHOV. Careful, Nadiezhda, we don't want to get drunk, do we.

NADIEZHDA. Do you have to be so vulgar? You make it sound like I've been drunk before. What are you doing carrying that silly little stick around?

MONAKHOV. I intend to play it in a moment.

PRITYKIN. (*Taking* MONAKHOV *by the arm.*) Come on, let's go watch the Chief of Police play his trumps. (*They go inside,* MONAKHOV *reluctantly.*)

TSYGANOV. (*Handing* NEDIEZHDA *her drink.*) I take it you don't like the clarinet.

NADIEZHDA. I like the guitar. The guitar moves me. A clarinet always sounds like it has a cold. You drink an awful lot, Doctor.

DR. MAKAROV. My name is Pavel Ivanich.

TSYGANOV. You know, that's the first time I've actually heard your name, isn't that odd?

DR. MAKAROV. No one here exists, why should they have a name.

TSYGANOV. You're always so lugubrious, my dear Pavel Ivanich.

DR. MAKAROV. Not everybody finds it easy to laugh in a mortuary.

CHERKOON. (*Calling, off.*) Sergei! Lydia Pavlovna wants you in here.

TSYGANOV. Excuse me . . . coming! (TSYGANOV *goes into the house.*)

DR. MAKAROV. (*Looking gloomily at* NADIEZHDA.) You like him, don't you?

NADIEZHDA. He's nice to talk to. He's interesting. And he knows how to dress.

DR. MAKAROV. (*In a quiet, muffled voice.*) He's a swine. He's trying to seduce you . . . and he'll do it, too . . . the swine.

NADIEZHDA. (*Calm.*) You're always insulting everyone. You shouldn't. If you kept your mouth shut people wouldn't be able to see how bad your teeth are.

DR. MAKAROV. (*Passionately, with pain.*) Nadiezhda, I can't stand it, seeing you with these people. It's killing me. I beg you, with all my heart and soul, go away, leave them, they're greedy, they're insatiable . . . nothing is enough for them, Nadiezhda, they'll devour everything in sight, everything.

NADIEZHDA. (*Standing up.*) Doctor, we don't know each other. You have no right to talk to me like this.

DR. MAKAROV. Don't go, please. Listen to me, Nadiezhda, I'm the only one that sees what you're really worth, you're like the earth itself, you have life inside you, hidden oceans of love! Give me just one tiny part of it. You don't know . . . the way I love you . . . it's crippling . . . but if you let me I could love you like a fire . . . and forever.

NADIEZHDA. Good heavens! But . . . but what if I don't find you at all attractive. I mean, look at yourself . . . how could you be anyone's lover. This is ridiculous.

DR. MAKAROV. Just wait, you'll see. I'll lie down in your path. Wherever you turn I'll be there. You've already killed one man, I'll be the second. The minute I see that that degenerate has had his way with you . . .

NADIEZHDA. (*With slight irritation.*) Now, really, stop being stupid. How could he have his way with me when I don't want him to, and anyway, it's none of your business. You can be very annoying, you know . . . unbearable, in fact. (VESYOLKINA *runs in.*)

VESYOLKINA. Did you hear the news? Guess who arrived, completely unexpected, Anna Fyodorovna. Isn't that incredible? Maybe they were never really separated. Maybe they're getting back together. Then what'll he do about Lydia Pavlovna . . . he's in love with her, you know. (*The* DOCTOR *walks away from the table and glowers at* NADIEZHDA.)

NADIEZHDA. (*Slowly.*) That's interesting. Except I don't believe he's in love with Lydia Pavlovna.

VESYOLKINA. What do you mean? The whole town knows that!

NADIEZHDA. How could they? You can't see love. Love is concealed within the heart.

VESYOLKINA. And the eyes and the voice . . . ?

NADIEZHDA. (*Thoughtfully.*) But why did she come back . . . his wife. What does she want? I mean she's not a dangerous rival, but still . . .

DR. MAKAROV. A dangerous rival for who?

NADIEZHDA. (*After a pause, slowly.*) It's none of your business.

VESYOLKINA. (*To* DOC.) Are you all right? You look . . .

DR. MAKAROV. (*Like an echo.*) It's none of your business.

VESYOLKINA. (*To* DOC.) Very funny. (*To* NADIEZHDA.) Let's go see what *is* going on. (*She and* NADIEZHDA *exit.* MONAKHOV *appears from among the trees and goes up to the* DOCTOR *with a smile.*)

MONAKHOV. Well, my friend, how goes it?

DR. MAKAROV. You've asked me that brilliant question a hundred times. What do you want to know exactly. Well?

MONAKHOV. Shhhh. You don't have to bite my head off. I don't want to know anything. I know everything I need to know.

DR. MAKAROV. (*Spitefully.*) Do you know that I . . . that I love your wife?

MONAKHOV. (*Quietly, mockingly.*) My friend, everyone knows that.

DR. MAKAROV. (*About to leave.*) In that case you can go to hell.

MONAKHOV. (*Grabbing his sleeve.*) Now look, let's not fight, eh? "Life's too short" as the poet says . . . and, anyway, I hate a scene.

DR. MAKAROV. (*Abruptly, quietly.*) What do you want?

MONAKHOV. (*Mysteriously.*) I want her to experience sorrow . . . to suffer a blow . . . but not from me! And not from you, either, my friend. You're just . . . I feel sorry for you. After all, I'm a kindhearted man and I see what's going on. I see everything. Everything. One cruel blow and she'll soften. Suffering does that. Makes people softer. Do you understand what I'm saying?

DR. MAKAROV. You're drunk.

MONAKHOV. I've been drinking, yes, who hasn't been drinking. It's nice, isn't it . . . feels good.

DR. MAKAROV. (*Angrily.*) You're poisonous. You're repulsive. (*The* DOCTOR *walks away quickly.* MONAKHOV *goes to the table, a pitiful, strange smile on his face. He drinks some wine and mutters.*)

MONAKHOV. Yes . . . yes, my friend, it hurts. You think it doesn't hurt me? (*Enter* PELEGAYA, *followed by* DROBYAZGIN *and* VESYOLKINA.)

PELAGEYA. Marvriky Osipovich, have you heard the news?

MONAKHOV. What news?

PELAGEYA. Cherkoon's wife . . . she's come back.

MONAKHOV. Already? Well, they usually do. And, tell me, what is the appropriate response to this great event?

PELAGEYA. Haven't you seen what's been going on?

VESYOLKINA. He's fallen in love with Lydia Pavlovna.

DROBYAZGIN. I think they're perfect for each other.

MONAKHOV. Good. Then everything's fine.

PELAGEYA. What's fine about it? (DROBYAZGIN *glances around, takes a pear from the table and sneaks a bite from it.*)

MONAKHOV. Everything. They're perfect for each other, his wife's come back, you're all wonderful people and I'm a good man. The main thing is not to interfere. (*He laughs and exits.*)

PELAGEYA. It's true, he is a good man, but he doesn't understand very much.

VESYOLKINA. He doesn't have time to, he has to keep an eye on his wife.

DROBYAZGIN. Nadiezhda Polikarpovna isn't that kind of a woman.

VESYOLKINA. Oh what do you know about it anyway. She's just waiting for someone to come along so she can fall in love.

DROBYAZGIN. Everybody's waiting for that. Even rabbits.

PELAGEYA. It's true, that's what everyone wants.

VESYOLKINA. Pelageya Ivanovna, do you love your husband?

PELAGEYA. Very much. But does he love me? Not very much. It's my own fault. They say you should never rob the cradle. (*Enter* BOGAYEVSKAYA, GRISHA, REDOZUBOV *and* PAVLIN. DROBYAZGIN *draws himself up and assumes a deferential air.* GRISHA *makes faces at him in a friendly way.* VESYOLKINA *notices this and laughs.*)

PAVLIN. So I said to her, "The covent," I said, "that's the easy way, but if you took responsibility for that poor old father of yours, if you brought some warmth into his life . . . now there's true penance, there's a proper cross to bear."

REDOZUBOV. You hear that, Grisha?

GRISHA. Don't look at me. I didn't say I was going to a convent.

REDOZUBOV. Acch, you damn fool.

PELAGEYA. Tatiana Nikolayevna. And this is such a wonderful birthday party . . . did I congratulate you? Plenty of everything and all of it so delicious, all these delicacies. I can't tell you how nice it is to be here.

BOGAYEVSKAYA. Well, I'm glad you're enjoying yourself. If only it weren't so hot.

PELAGEYA. Sergei Nikolayich taught me just the thing for hot weather. Lemonade and brandy. It's really refreshing. You should try some.

REDOZUBOV. Tatiana Bogayevskaya, why did you have to invite me here. I could be sitting comfortably at home right now but you send Pavlin over, "Please, Mr. Mayor, you have to come", that's what he tells me. . . .

BOGAYEVSKAYA. If you don't like it, leave your children here and go home.

REDOZUBOV. (*Thoughtfully.*) He has me on a leash, that Cherkoon. On a leash. Everything he tells me to do, I do it. Me. Redozubov.

BOGAYEVSKAYA. And a good thing, too. He stops you from doing stupid things. You should have been put on a leash ages ago.

REDOZUBOV. I've had my pillars broken up . . . seven years I fought for them . . . all that money down the drain . . .

PAVLIN. It's a shame about the pillars. They greatly enhanced the local architecture.

BOGAYEVSKAYA. Nonsense . . .

PAVLIN. The only problem is how they made driving a little difficult . . . other than that . . . And people used to ask, you know, when they saw them they'd say "Who do these pillars belong to?" And then they'd find out that Verkhopolye had a mayor called Redozubov.

REDOZUBOV. Grisha! Get away from those bottles.

GRISHA. I was just looking.

BOGAYEVSKAYA. Why do you have to yell at him? You turn him into an imbecile and then you yell at him for acting like one.

REDOZUBOV. You think I don't see what's going on here? These anacrists . . . they're barbarians, that's what they are, they destroy everything, they tear it down. The whole town's falling apart and it's all their fault.

BOGAYEVSKAYA. (*Yawning.*) Must have been badly built in the first place.

REDOZUBOV. You're a lady, what do you care? You're all the same, you lah-de-dah people . . . you didn't make anything by yourself, you used other people's hands, that's why you don't care. It's us that did the work. We broke our backs, we did . . .

BOGAYEVSKAYA. You did. But at least we're not greedy. What we had made was made well and it's still standing. When you die all you'll leave behind is a barren patch of earth that you plundered and picked clean.

REDOZUBOV. (*Angrily.*) Grisha! Get away, don't you touch those bottles. Where's Katya? (*Enter the* CHIEF OF POLICE *and* PRITIKIN.) Tell your sister to come home. Go on. Here's Pritikin. Is he better than me? But look at the way they treat him. (REDOZUBOV *exits with* PAVLIN.)

BOGAYEVSKAYA. I shouldn't have been so sharp with the poor old thing. I am a fool.

PELAGEYA. But, my dear, the way he was carrying on.

CHIEF OF POLICE. Tatiana Nikolayevna, your house is the Garden of Eden and you are the Goddess of Light.

BOGAYEVSKAYA. Oh, yes, the spitting image, no doubt.

CHIEF OF POLICE. And so, dear goddess, let me wish you another fifty happy returns at the very least.

BOGAYEVSKAYA. That's a few too many, I think.

PRITYKIN. But you know something, it's true, Tatiana Nilolayevna. Anywhere else Redozubov would have chewed my head off, but in your house he behaves himself. Everyone respects you . . . everyone behaves well under your roof.

BOGAYEVSKAYA. (*Calmly.*) They know I can show them the door.

CHIEF OF POLICE. Bravo . . . !

PRITYKIN. (*Enthusiastically.*) Three cheers for the door!

PELAGEYA. (*Sighs.*) It's a good thing when someone knows they can be shown the door.

PRITYKIN. (*To* PELAGAYA, *provocatively and with meaning.*) Who are you talking about?

PELAGEYA. I'm just . . . in general. You didn't think I meant you?

PRITYKIN. Just watch what you're saying.

CHIEF OF POLICE. At ease, men. Now then, the drink's been drunk, the food's been ett . . . what's next on the agenda?

PRITYKIN. Gin rummy.

PELAGEYA. Even I know how to play that.

CHIEF OF POLICE. If you'll excuse me . . .

BOGAYEVSKAYA. Please, please . . . run along. (*All go out, except* BOGAYEVSKAYA, *who sits in a chair and fans herself with a handkerchief.* MATVEY *is hanging up the lanterns and adjusting them.* STEPAN *and* KATYA *appear together.* STEPAN *is talking with his usual mocking edge.*)

STEPAN. That's the only place to be. Where else is the great fire of reason burning? That's where all the honest and intelligent people are, the ones who really see what's going on in this country . . . what a horrible and squalid mess it is.

KATYA. (*Softly.*) Are there really a lot of honest and intelligent people there?

STEPAN. (*With a laugh.*) Well, not that many ... (BOGAYEVSKAYA *laughs softly.*) But that's why I'm saying you should go there. Now, while you're young. Two or three years, that's all. Throw a part of yourself into the fire, see what it's like to dream about a new kind of life, to join in the protest against lies and corruption ...

KATYA. (*Simply.*) I'll go.

STEPAN. Of course you may find it frightening ... you may end up running back to this swamp, but still, at least you'll have done something with your youth ... something you can remember ... and that's worth whatever you may have to pay for it.

KATYA. I'll never come back.

STEPAN. All the things that are going on in the world and not a whisper of it ever reaches this godforsaken backwater. Look at them ... look at how blind and deaf and stupid they all are.

KATYA. (*With a shudder.*) Monakhov and the Doctor ... they're like frogs ...

STEPAN. Yes, and what could ever happen to you here? End up married to some merchant ... someone like your brother ... (STEPAN *sees* BOGAYEVSKAYA, *is slightly embarrassed.*)

BOGAYEVSKAYA. Well, young man, no need to be embarrassed. He's talking well, Katya ... straightforward and no promises. When he starts making promises, be careful.

STEPAN. (*Not polite but very sincere.*) You're fantastic. You're an incredible woman.

BOGAYEVSKAYA. Never mind about that. Well, don't stand around here, get on with it. (*Exit* STEPAN *and* KATYA.) Oh, you dear creatures. (LYDIA *enters reading a note, agitated.*) Lyduchka.

BARBARIANS

LYDIA. Oh, so there you are. Fed up with all the company.

BOGAYEVSKAYA. At my age it doesn't take much to make you fed up. Lydia . . . sit down. I have something to tell you. You know, I've lived out here in the wilds for thirteen years, never once poked my nose out into the civilised world, so I'm afraid I've become a bit of a savage myself. There's all sorts of things I just don't understand any more, so forgive me if this is none of my business . . .

LYDIA. You don't have to. Cherkoon and me . . . that's what you mean, isn't it?

BOGAYEVSKAYA. Yes, that. Tongues are wagging, you know.

LYDIA. Are we supposed to care about that?

BOGAYEVSKAYA. No, I suppose not. Well, then, there's nothing more to say.

LYDIA. (*Thoughtfully.*) Here . . . if you're interested . . . she sent me this note, his wife . . . she says she's "without animosity" . . . something like that. My god people are pitiful, aren't they.

BOGAYEVSKAYA. People? Perhaps. But I do feel sorry for her.

LYDIA. (*Smiling.*) Don't worry. I wouldn't steal a beggar's last crust.

BOGAYEVSKAYA. Lydochka, not really. You're a Bogayevskaya. You know your own worth, I'm sure. Well, I've had a little rest now, I'd better go back inside. Tell me one thing. Do you like him?

LYDIA. Not especially. But compared to the others . . .

BOGAYEVSKAYA. Yes, but he's so ill-mannered. Well, God send you happiness.

LYDIA. Oh, auntie, if it's there and I see it, I'll take it without his help.

BOGAYEVSKAYA. (*Quietly.*) They're coming.

LYDIA. Why are you whispering? (*Enter* ANNA, NADIEZHDA, *and* CHERKOON.)

BOGAYEVSKAYA. Good evening, Anna Fyodorovna, how nice to see you. It's my birthday, and here you are.

ANNA. (*Nervously excited.*) Many happy returns . . . good evening Lydia Pavlovna. (LYDIA *shakes her hands and smiles.*) It's so strange to be here. I've been living in the middle of the woods for the past two months. Totally isolated. I've hardly seen a soul, and now suddenly here I am . . . all this excitement . . . it makes me dizzy.

CHERKOON. (*Frowning.*) Why don't you have a rest.

ANNA. Later. Where's Katya?

NADIEZHDA. (*To* LYDIA.) Anna Fyodorovna's become so beautiful, look at her.

LYDIA. She always was.

KATYA. (*Running in.*) Here you are! Oh, I'm so happy to see you. But look how thin you are, and your eyes . . . (*They embrace.* CHERKOON *frowns.* NADIEZHDA *is watching him and* LYDIA *carefully.* VESYOLKINA *and* MONAKHOV *are in the bushes.*)

ANNA. What about them?

KATYA. They're so serious . . . so sad . . .

ANNA. And you, how are you doing?

KATYA. Oh, I'm fine. It's very interesting, you know, Stepan's still taking me on those long walks . . . my father hates it, you should hear him carry on. Stepan's so clever, but he always lectures me like I was a little girl . . . he's much better with the peasants . . . he knows how to talk to them. Oh, let's go for a walk, can we . . . ?

ANNA. (*Moving away with her.*) He's a peasant himself, you know, that's why. (ANNA *and* KATYA *exit.* TSYGANOV *enters.* CHERKOON *watches his wife.* MONAKHOV *grins at him from the bushes. The* DOCTOR *is standing in the background.* LYDIA *peels a pear, humming.*)

BARBARIANS

CHERKOON. What are you doing out here?

TSYGANOV. Nadiezhda Polikarpovna disappeared, and what am I away from her but a man adrift.

NADIEZHDA. You're very good at compliments. One can't even tell what they mean half the time.

TSYGANOV. Thank you for the compliment.

NADIEZHDA. Yegor Petrovich never says nice things to me. (LYDIA *goes into the house.*)

TSYGANOV. That's because he's a savage. No breeding at all.

NADIEZHDA. Mavriky, what are you doing there?

MONAKHOV. I've found a spider.

NADIEZHDA. Oh, don't, it's disgusting.

MONAKHOV. Not at all. I like to observe. You can learn a great deal sometimes just by watching.

NADIEZHDA. What can you possibly learn from a spider?

MONAKHOV. He's caught a ladybug . . . not a very big one, but it's bigger than him . . . he can't handle it. First he fiddled around with it for a moment then he went to get help. Now he's talking to a neighbor. "Help me kill it", he says, "and I'll let you eat some of it yourself." (*The* DOCTOR *speaks from the distance, sharply and without expression.*)

DR. MAKAROV. That's you, Monakhov, you're describing yourself. (*The* DOCTOR *walks away.*)

TSYGANOV. What was that all about?

NADIEZHDA. God, he frightened me.

MONAKHOV. He's been drinking. Drink makes him philosophic. (MONAKHOV *walks away.*)

CHIEF OF POLICE. That doctor's an incredibly rude man.

TSYGANOV. Hark, the gentle red-head speaks.

NADIEZHDA. He's just telling the truth, and that's a good thing. Yegor Petrovich always says beautiful things.

TSYGANOV. Georges, there's no way round it, you and I are going to have to fight a duel. Let's get away from him, he has a bad effect on my nervous system. Your arm, dear goddess, we shall walk in the garden and speak of love. (*They move off together.*)

NADIEZHDA. Yegor Petrovich never talks about love.

TSYGANOV. A man with ice in his heart.

NADIEZHDA. I don't agree. I love the way you call him Georges. It fits him . . . Georges . . . ! (*They exit. CHERKOON, worried, drums his fingers on the table and whistles shrilly. Enter ANNA, KATYA and STEPAN. From inside the house comes the triumphant voice of PELAGEYA. By the time ANNA starts talking about children the CHIEF OF POLICE and PRITIKIN have arrived at the table. GRISHA, his lips moving, is reading the labels on the bottles with fierce concentration.*)

PRITIKIN. I told that old scoundrel a thing or two, oh yes I did. That Redozubov won't forget me in a hurry. He knows who he's dealing with now. (*Laughs loudly.*)

ANNA. I've only been gone for two months, but it feels like years. The things I saw in the countryside . . . it was frightening.

STEPAN. Yes, it's no joke, is it.

ANNA. You wouldn't believe it, Katya . . . men who beat their wives . . . they enjoy it . . . actually enjoy it, hitting them in the face with a closed fist, beating them until they bleed and then kicking them with their feet . . . you have no idea.

KATYA. (*Pause.*) I do. Papa used to beat my mother. He beats Grisha.

ANNA. Oh god, you poor darling . . .

CHERKOON. Anna, don't excite yourself.

STEPAN. It's funny to hear you talking. It's like you didn't have eyes until yesterday.

ANNA. The children are the worst . . . they're so upsetting to see. They're all suffering from some disease . . . and they're totally neglected. Their eyes are hollow and they look frightened all the time . . . the mothers beat them and curse them because they were born sick. If only people could see what their lives are like.

PRITYKIN. We see. Oh, of course it's all strange and new to you, but not to us. We know the villagers are wild animals, we know that, and it's getting worse and worse every year. The women aren't so bad maybe, but the men, they belong in prison, every last one of them.

MONAKHOV. The women are just as bad. Who sells the illegal vodka that makes the men drunk and violent in the first place?

CHIEF OF POLICE. Exactly . . . and d'you know how the women take care of their husbands? They bake a special treat for supper . . . cabbage pie laced with arsenic, good-bye, husband. That's right.

KATYA. (*Heatedly.*) What else can they do? Their husbands beat them all the time. Serves them right.

PELAGEYA. (*Timedly.*) Oh my god, she can't mean that.

CHIEF OF POLICE. (*Jovially.*) Now now, careful what you say around me . . .

KATYA. Uggg, stop breathing all over me.

ANNA. (*Bewildered.*) I don't understand . . . if you know all this about life here . . .

CHERKOON. Don't be naive, Anna.

STEPAN. (*With a smile.*) Which one of us did you expect to be surprised?

KATYA. What are you grinning at? You're always grinning at everything . . . what's so funny?

STEPAN. This country's rotten with crime . . . crimes there aren't even names for. You can't touch the criminals because they're in power and they're the ones that make the laws in the first place. And what are you doing about all this? You're sitting in a garden going oh and ah, how terrible, how terrible . . . (*The* CHIEF OF POLICE *takes* PRITIKIN's *arm and they go out together.*)

KATYA. Well, what is to be done, tell us?

ANNA. Yes, what? (GRISHA *looks around, takes a bottle and walks off with it.*)

STEPAN. Only one thing you can do. Try to open people's eyes. Teach the blind to see. That's all.

CHERKOON. Modern communications, that's the answer. Highways. Railroads; iron rails are the only thing that'll cut through this mess.

STEPAN. Iron rails? Iron people is what we really need. Our kind will never manage it. Look at us . . . we already know what's obsolete and we can't let go of it, it's too close to us, it's in our blood. Obviously we're not the ones that'll build a new world, and the sooner we realise it, the better. Put us all in our place.

MONAKHOV. (*To* KATYA.) Your little brother's just absconded with a bottle of chartreuse. Look, there he is, guzzling away . . .

KATYA. Oh, you fool . . .

GRISHA. (*Off.*) It's none of your business. Let go, get off me, it's mine . . . you can't have it . . . (STEPAN *goes off towards the noise.*)

STEPAN. He'll break her head open. . . .

MONAKHOV. Powerful stuff, chartreuse.

ANNA. I see Sergei Nikolayich is still educating him.

CHERKOON. I doubt that Sergei taught him to steal bottles.

ANNA. Didn't he teach him to drink? (*She looks around and, seeing that they are alone, begins talking fast and nervously.*) Yegor, I want you to know . . . I've come back here to be with you.

CHERKOON. Please, Anna, not now.

ANNA. No, wait, let me explain. I've acepted the idea that you and I . . . that we're strangers . . . that I'm a stranger to you, anyway.

CHERKOON. (*Quietly, mocking.*) A stranger? Why, what was it that made us close before . . . was it just kisses, nothing else?

ANNA. (*With pain.*) No. I don't know. All I know for sure is . . . life without you . . . it's unbearable. On my own I just feel so stupid all the time . . . so useless. I don't know anything, I can't do anything . . .

CHERKOON. Anna, just tell me what you want, just tell me simply, what is it you want?

ANNA. Please, don't be cruel. I didn't come back to beg. I love you, yes, I do love you very deeply, Yegor, but I know it's useless . . . I know it's useless if you've decided . . .

CHERKOON. (*In a hollow voice.*) Why, Anna, why do we have to tear and scratch at each other like this?

ANNA. I know my love isn't a very important thing, Yegor, but it does torture me, I can't help it . . . no, don't go, please! I'm ashamed of myself . . . that I can't get over this . . . I was hurt and offended when I went away. I thought about death . . .

CHERKOON. (*Gloomily.*) Anna, I don' know what to say to you. I don't understand you, I've never understood you . . .

ANNA. (*With fear.*) I'm helpless on my own, I feel worthless and frightened all the time, I'm afraid of everything . . . I see one of those sick, beaten children and I just burst out crying, I can't control it . . .

CHERKOON. (*Firmly.*) Anna, I'm sorry, you'll have to tell me what it is you want from me.

ANNA. I want . . . I just want to be near you . . . just

for now, for a little longer. I won't get in your way. You can live exactly as you want only let me, please let me be near you.

CHERKOON. Don't you see how painful that would be for you? (*Enter* KATYA.)

ANNA. (*With a pale smile.*) If it is I'll go away again. I will. Don't you see . . . I'm helpless . . . I don't understand anything about life, I never thought seriously about anything until now . . . teach me, Yegor, please . . .

KATYA. What are you two talking about?

ANNA. About life, my dear. (*To* CHERKOON.) You owe me that much for everything you've taken.

CHERKOON. I don't know, Anna. How can I do that? This is so awkward . . .

KATYA. Oh, it's so awkward, poor you. (*Stamping foot.*) Ooooow, I hate men. Someday I'll teach that Stepan Lukin a thing or two.

ANNA. (*With a smile.*) I'm embarrassed that I'm the way I am. But where can I turn? There's no one. I can't go home. My family's still living in another century, grumbling all the time because the world keeps changing around them, self righteous and angry about everything new. Same old furniture, same old books, same old fashioned ways . . . it's so bleak and haunted at home. You know, sometimes they get frightened suddenly for no reason at all, and they start talking about how life cheated them . . . and then other times they'll just walk around in a dream, living off their memories. . . . (TSYGANOV *and* NADIEZHDA *return and go to the table.* TSYGANOV *pours himself some wine.*) Since I've known you I've grown so far away from them. I don't understand them at all.

TSYGANOV. (*To* NADIEZHDA.) Being with you is two

things, my dear. It's a pleasure . . . and it's terrifying. Like standing at the edge of a cliff.

NADIEZHDA. You drink much to much. . . .

KATYA. Have you two made up?

CHERKOON. Don't tell her, Anna. Let her die of curiosity.

KATYA. I can tell anyway. Oh, if you were my husband I swear I'd grab on to you like this . . . (*She clenches her fist.*)

CHERKOON. Are you trying to scare me, young lady?

ANNA. Dear, dear Katya. (MONAKHOV *appears among the trees.*)

TSYGANOV. The sad thing is, I aim my shafts of love at your heart but they just glance off and fall to the ground. It's such a pity, really.

ANNA. (*Quickly.*) Let's get away from here, Katya. (*She takes* KATYA *by the arm.*)

KATYA. Not back inside, though. Let's go to the summer house. (*They exit.* CHERKOON *heads back towards the house.*)

CHERKOON. (*With a laugh.*) You're making your business a bit public, Sergei.

TSYGANOV. Ah, Georges, what do I care? Let the world look on, let it shudder with envy.

NADIEZHDA. (*Thoughtfully.*) Georges . . . that's such a nice name. Mavriky, what are you doing there? (MONAKHOV *enters, nods towards the table.*)

MONAKHOV. Just . . . on my way to the table. . . .

NADIEZHDA. You were not. You were spying on me.

MONAKHOV. (*Brusquely.*) Grumbling again. What is it this time . . . stomach ache, or is it your corns acting up.

NADIEZHDA. (*To* TSY.) You see, he always does that. He deliberately says vulgar disgusting things about me in front of men so they won't find me attractive.

TSYGANOV. Really . . . an interesting technique.

NADIEZHDA. (*Sincerely and simply.*) If you only knew how horrible he is. Sometimes he says my breath smells . . .

MONAKHOV. (*Alarmed.*) What?! Nadya, what are you talking about, when did I ever say that?

NADIEZHDA. (*Pursuing him.*) You need reminding, I'll remind you . . .

MATVEY. (*Stepping back.*) Oh, Nadya, calm down, I was only joking . . . (MONAKHOV *and* NADIEZHDA *pass tree. They disappear into the bushes.* TSYGANOV *sits down wearily in an armchair. His face is sad.* DROBYAZGIN *and* GRISHA *come up to the table.*)

DROBYAZGIN. Sergei Nikolayich, is it all right if I ask you something? What are the "secret vices"?

TSYGANOV. That I shall never tell you, my friend. I like you just the way you are, vices right out in the open. It's more aesthetically satisfying.

DROBYAZGIN. Well, is there any such thing as the "secret virtues"?

TSYGANOV. That's the only kind there are. Have you ever seen a virtue out in the open?

GRISHA. What's it called again, that thick green stuff you gave me the first time? Do you remember?

TSYGANOV. Chartreuse . . . Repeat after me . . . chartreuse. . . . (GRISHA *repeats the name in a low voice and smiles.* MATVEY *lights lanterns in the garden.*)

DROBYAZGIN. Sergei Nikolayich, who was the wisest of all the wise men that ever lived.

TSYGANOV. Ah, now there's an interesting question . . . which philosophers generally answer with the following story. Once upon a time there were three wise men. The first believed that the world was made only of thought. The second believed just the opposite . . . whatever that might be, don't remember. But what we do know for a fact is that the third wise man seduced the wife of the first, stole a manuscript from the second, had it published under his own name and was crowned with laurels.

GRISHA. (*Delighted.*) Pretty smart.

DROBYAZGIN. (*Doubtful.*) Hmmmm, yes, but it sounds a little dishonest to me.

TSYGANOV. Dishonest! Worse than that, it was downright naughty. And now, let's drink to youth. How sad that a man never knows until too late how wonderful it is to be young, like Grisha here. (LYDIA *stands with a flower in her hand and looks with disapproval at the drinking.*)

DROBYAZGIN. Sergei Nikolayich, do you think there'll always be thieves and robbers in the world?

TSYGANOV. Yes, of course. That is until one day a man comes along, the biggest thief ever, and he'll steal everything there is to steal, which will leave nothing, and at that moment the world will become honest.

GRISHA. (*Laughing.*) And then there won't even be any clothes left so everyone'll have to go around naked! (*Laughs.*)

LYDIA. Uncle Serge . . .

TSYGANOV. What can I do for you, my dear? (DROBYAZGIN *and* GRISHA *withdraw respectfully.*)

LYDIA. Why do you lead them along like this?

TSYGANOV. Why not? It's fun, corrupting those two little piggies a bit. Who knows, maybe with a touch of vice here and there they'll pass for human beings.

LYDIA. Sergei Tsyganov, bon vivant and social lion, holding court with . . . with what?

TSYGANOV. And in love with the tax collector's wife.

Yes, things could certainly be better. The world is out of joint, definitely . . . definitely . . .

LYDIA. Sergei, what's the matter . . . tell me.

TSYGANOV. That woman . . . that damn woman.

LYDIA. You're not serious.

TSYGANOV. Yes.

BOGAYEVSKAYA. (*Calling, off.*) Sergei Nikolayich . . . !

TSYGANOV. Coming! You know, I'm thinking quite seriously about asking her to join with me in holy matrimony. As the shopkeepers say, "It's time I was taken off the shelf." Are you coming in?

LYDIA. No, it's too depressing, watching all of you. It makes me want to leave here tomorrow.

TSYGANOV. Because someone returned unexpectedly today?

LYDIA. Do you have to be vulgar with me too? (TSYGANOV *shrugs and goes out.* LYDIA *goes to exit* R., *humming softly.* ANNA *comes to meet her, walking quickly.*)

ANNA. Did you get my note?

LYDIA. Yes. Was it really necessary?

ANNA. Were you offended?

LYDIA. It seems to me you're just humiliating yourself.

ANNA. I don't care. I love him.

LYDIA. Is there something you want to say to me?

ANNA. (*Anxiously, with pain.*) Yes . . . please try to understand . . . I don't like myself very much right now . . . I just have to be with him, I can't manage on my own, it's too overwhelming, everything, I only feel alive when I'm near him.

LYDIA. (*Coldly.*) Do I have to hear this?

ANNA. Please, listen to me. You're stronger than I am, you should try to be kind. There's something I want to ask . . . but I don't know how. You know what it is, don't you?

LYDIA. Yes, I think so. You want to know if I love your husband, is that it? No, I don't. (GRISHA *comes cautiously to the table, takes a bottle of wine and disappears.*)

ANNA. Is that the truth? (*She grabs* LYDIA's *hand.*) And him . . . does he love you? Please, tell me.

LYDIA. I don't know. I don't think so, not really.

ANNA. (*With pain.*) But you must know that!

LYDIA. We're friends. We enjoy talking to each other.

ANNA. (*With pride.*) Well, there's things I can talk about now, too. Things I've seen.

LYDIA. (*Smiling.*) Well, that's very good.

ANNA. (*With sincerity.*) You find me pathetic, don't you? But I just don't know how to live without him . . . I can't help myself. . . .

LYDIA. I'm sorry but . . . it seems to me . . . perhaps your kind of love . . . it's a burden for him.

ANNA. No, he's strong. He's very strong.

LYDIA. Good-bye. (*She exits.*)

ANNA. Don't despise me . . . please. It doesn't matter. Nothing matters any more. Oh, lord, help me . . . help me. (*Enter* CHIEF OF POLICE, *and* PRITIKIN, *both very drunk.* ANNA *sees them and hurries away.*)

CHIEF OF POLICE. Put yourself in my place Arkhip. You're the Chief of Police, all right, and you decide it's time you got married. But there's one problem. Who should you marry. That's the question, you see . . . who?

PRITYKIN. First of all, someone with money.

CHIEF OF POLICE. Of course, goes without saying. But what if they both have money? Nadiezhda Polikarpovna. Lydia Pavlovna. Which one would you choose?

PRITYKIN. I'd take Lydia Pavlovna.
CHIEF OF POLICE. Mmmm, yes, maybe. But why her?
PRITYKIN. Because Nakiezhda's married. Anyway, about that student, let me tell you what he's been telling the peasants. . . .
CHIEF OF POLICE. To hell with him. To hell with the student. Now you've made a good point. Nadiezhda's married . . . that's a good point. But what if she became a widow? It could happen, you know. . . .
PRITYKIN. That can happen to any woman.
CHIEF OF POLICE. (*Astonished.*) Any woman . . . absolutely . . . any woman can become a widow. My god, don't you see it? That means we'll all die one day. You see what I'm getting at. Dead!
PRITYKIN. That's how it usually ends up.
CHIEF OF POLICE. Ends up. You old devil. Ends down is more like it. You end up down and you stay down.
PRITYKIN. The things that student's been saying . . .
CHIEF OF POLICE. (*Thoughtfully.*) Other people are out in the woods hunting, or inside playing cards, but you're lying under the earth, dead.
PRITYKIN. You should pay more attention to him. Maybe he's just a student but he's been telling the peasants they've paid for everything with their own blood. . . .
CHIEF OF POLICE. Ridiculous . . . (*Enter* DROBYAZGIN, *running.*)
PRITYKIN. No, it's true. He's a dangerous cancer in this town.
DROBYAZGIN. Yakov Alexeyich, we need you inside. The doctor just hit Monakhov in the face.
CHIEF OF POLICE. What? Why did he do that?

BARBARIANS

DROBYAZGIN. I don't know. (*The three of them go inside.* DUNYA'S HUSBAND *appears behind the trees, wildly drunk and clothes in tatters.* CHERKOON *leads the* DOCTOR *in by the arm, followed by* NADIEZHDA *and then* STYOPA.)

CHERKOON. You'd better get out of here right away.

DR. MAKAROV. (*Bellowing.*) Who the hell are you? It's your fault anyway. You started everything. . . .

CHERKOON. (*Quietly.*) Shut up, you damned fool. You should be ashamed of yourself.

DR. MAKAROV. You're vultures, that's what you are, a pair of vultures. Well, I'm not some dead carcass lying on the ground, you're not going to pick me clean like you did old Redozubov. Who the hell do you think you are, that's what I'd like to know.

CHERKOON. Come on . . . come on, let's go . . . this way . . . (*He takes the* DOCTOR *to the end of the garden.*)

NADIEZHDA. (*Joyfully, to* STYOPA.) Did you see that? Did you see how he handled the doctor? Just took him by the arm and led him away. He's not afraid of anything. (*She follows* CHERKOON *out.*)

STYOPA. (*Shouts.*) Yegor Petrovich! (*She has seen her father and is frightened and angry.*) What are you doing here? Go away. What do you want?

DUNYA'S HUSBAND. Stepinida . . . I'm your father, aren't I? Therefore . . . come with me.

STYOPA. No, I won't. I don't want to. Get away from me, I'm staying right here.

DUNYA'S HUSBAND. Then I'll get the police and they'll make you come.

STYOPA. I'll kill myself first. (*Enter* CHERKOON, NADIEZHDA, ANNA, LYDIA *and* TSYGANOV.) You hear me. You're not my father. You're nothing. You're a disease.

CHERKOON. You again. What do you want now?

DUNYA'S HUSBAND. I've come for my daughter.

STYOPA. No.

ANNA. Go inside, Styopa.

CHERKOON. And you get out . . . now.

DUNYA'S HUSBAND. If you're going to steal my daughter, you could at least give me a rouble. (STYOPA *grabs some money out of her pocket, throws the coins down and runs away.*)

STYOPA. There. Take it. I hope you choke to death on it.

CHERKOON. If I catch you around here again . . .

NADIEZHDA. Don't even talk to him . . .

CHERKOON. I'll handle this . . .

NADIEZHDA. You can't talk to a man like him. (*To* DUNYA'S HUSBAND.) You go away. I'll tell the Chief of Police tomorrow. He'll take care of you.

DUNYA'S HUSBAND. I'm not afraid of him. He can't do anything to me. I'm beyond it. (DUNYA'S HUSBAND *goes.*)

TSYGANOV. What a man, eh? Every day a little more of him. Growing like mould.

LYDIA. That's his power, having nothing to lose.

NADIEZHDA. (*To* CHERKOON.) You've had a hard day, haven't you? One thing after another.

ANNA. (*Involuntarily, like an echo.*) A hard day. Are you tired, Yegor?

CHERKOON. No, I'm just . . . I don't know what to do about that man. He has to stop bothering Styopa. It's getting me angry.

NADIEZHDA. You don't have to bother with it. I'll take care of it. You can't let it upset you.

TSYGANOV. My dear, I think it's your husband that's upset.

BARBARIANS

NADIEZHDA. (*Surprised.*) My husband?

CHERKOON. (*Sudden rage.*) He's like a mud puddle, your husband, you can't turn anywhere without stepping in him . . .

ANNA. (*Stunned, quietly.*) Yegor . . . stop.

TSYGANOV. (*With a laugh.*) He's not that bad, Georges.

CHERKOON. (*To* NADIEZHDA.) How can you stand it, having that slimey toad squatting around you all the time, I don't understand it.

TSYGANOV. (*Ironic.*) Bravo, Georges . . .

NADIEZHDA. (*Breathless with delight.*) He's wonderful, isn't he. (*To* TSY.) There's someone to be afraid of. There's a real man. It's true what he said. Every word of it.

ANNA. (*Anxiously, to* LYDIA.) My god she's strange. I mean don't you find her terribly strange?

LYDIA. Yes, I do. Let's go in.

NADIEZHDA. Why am I strange? Just because I value manliness more than anything. There's nothing strange about that.

CHERKOON. (*Embarrassed.*) Yes, well . . . um, I don't know anything about that. I think I'll go for a walk.

NADIEZHDA. Me too, I'll come with you. (*They exit.*)

ANNA. (*Anxiously, to* TSYGANOV.) She's so odd. I mean, she's nice enough, but she seems to be in another world.

TSYGANOV. (*To* ANNA.) Why don't you rest up. You've had a long journey . . . and all this confusion.

ANNA. Yes, I'll go and . . . no, but isn't she . . . I don't know . . . (ANNA *exits, quickly.* TSYGANOV *smokes and smiles. Drunken laughter and talk can be heard, then enter* MONAKHOV, DROBYAZGIN *and* GRISHA.)

LYDIA. (*With distaste.*) God, it's so unpleasant here. And that woman . . . well, both of them really, they're so pathetic. What are you laughing at?

TSYGANOV. Just thinking . . . what if she's finally found her hero.

LYDIA. (*Pause.*) I doubt it. No, no, that would be too ridiculous.

TSYGANOV. (*Laughing.*) What's ridiculous about it . . . ?

LYDIA. But why does he let himself get dragged down into all that . . . filth.

TSYGANOV. He doesn't 'let himself', it just happens. Naked instinct . . . dressed up by a trick of the mind . . . a few lofty words of love to make it all seem half-respectable. But underneath, pure lust, my dear. Remember?

MONAKHOV. All right, so he hit me, so what? I'm alive, aren't I? And he'll be dead soon, so who cares.

LYDIA. Here come the drunks. I'm going.

TSYGANOV. So am I.

GRISHA. I could bash someone's face in, too, I could, just like that, powee! (*They exit.* MONAKHOV *winks at his companions and makes a threatening gesture with his finger in the direction of* TSYGANOV. DROBYAZGIN *does not understand.*)

DROBYAZGIN. Why? He's all right. Has a real brain in his head.

MONAKHOV. So? What good is a brain? (*He laughs loudly.* DROBYAZGIN *and* GRISHA *break into laughter with him.*)

CURTAIN

ACT FOUR

A large, cosy sitting room. To the L. a door to the entrance hall and two windows; to the R. the door to ANNA's *room and another to* CHERKOON's. *At rear, large double doors to the drawing room, the corner of which protrudes into the sitting room. In an alcove between the projecting wall of the drawing room and Dutch Stove in the right corner is a sofa on which* TSYGANOV *lounges and smokes. To the right, between the doors is an upright piano on which* ANNA *plays, barely touching the keys.* BOGAYEVSKAYA *is sitting at a table in the middle of the room playing solitaire. In* CHERKOON's *room* STEPAN *goes over the books with an abacus.* CHERKOON *walks around the room absorbed in thought. He stops in front of the window, gazes out into the darkness.*

Evening.

The lamps are lit.

BOGAYEVSKAYA. It's getting chilly, isn't it?
ANNA. Would you like your shawl?
BOGAYEVSKAYA. Lydia's bringing it.
TSYGANOV. Stop that clicking in there.
STEPAN. I will . . . as soon as I catch him.
BOGAYEVSKAYA. Who are you chasing?
STEPHAN. Pritikin, the timber merchant.
BOGAYEVSKAYA. Has he been tampering with the books?

STEPAN. Diligently.

BOGAYEVSKAYA. A true businessman. Even when he's in love he can't help cheating.

TSYGANOV. Like ninety percent of mankind. Actually, I think it's a bad idea to expose swindlers. Just helps them hone their technique. Are you expecting someone, Yegor, you keep pacing?

CHERKOON. (*After a pause.*) So I'm pacing. What's it to you?

TSYGANOV. As the lawyers say, "No further question, you honor." I wish this weather would make up its mind.

ANNA. I think he was just upset by the argument.

CHERKOON. (*Coldly.*) You don't know what you're talking about.

ANNA. It seems to me that all this bad temper must be contagious. Two people start and pretty soon everybody's irritable.

CHERKOON. Congratulations. A remarkable observation. Very original.

BOGAYEVSKAYA. I thought it was quite interesting, that little argument they had. Well, perhaps interesting is the wrong word. No. Interesting. It was. Not that I understand these things . . .

CHERKOON. Lydia Pavlovna's not very subtle.

TSYGANOV. Unlike Georges here, subtlety personified.

BOGAYEVSKAYA. I'm going to miss all of you, really I am. It's a pity that you ever have to leave.

TSYGANOV. Why don't you come with us? After all, what can you do here?

BOGAYEVSKAYA. What can I do there? What can I do anywhere. Nothing. The very thing I've been doing all my life, a lifetime of nothing.

TSYGANOV. Well, at least that means you've done nothing wrong.

BOGAYEVSKAYA. (*Shuffling cards together.*) True, nothing wrong, nothing at all. This just isn't my day, Anna Fyodor'na. I haven't gotten through the deck once, not once.

ANNA. (*Sadly.*) No? That's too bad. I was hoping you'd be lucky this time.

BOGAYEVSKAYA. (*Dealing.*) Well, once more into the hands of fate.

STEPAN. (*In mock solemn tones.*) Never tamper with fate.

CHERKOON. (*Softly.*) It's fate that does the tampering.

STEPAN. And so does the nimble pen of our wily timber merchant.

BOGAYEVSKAYA. You get on with your clickety-click.

TSYGANOV. Till fate comes dancing clickety-click to your door. (LYDIA *enters with shawl.*)

BOGAYEVSKAYA. Ah, thank you, Lidusha. Have you heard about Pritikin? It seems he's romantically involved with Marie Vesyolkina, you know, from the post office.

LYDIA. Really? How fascinating.

BOGAYEVSKAYA. Well, it's something at least.

TSYGANOV. My dear Lydia, your problem is that nothing interests you . . . except riding. You lead a very strange life, you know, galloping across the fields on horseback, day and night, come rain or come shine, galloping away. There's more than that to life. There must be. It's amazing how you've changed.

LYDIA. For the worse?

TSYGANOV. Of course. What other way do we change?

LYDIA. Then there's nothing amazing about it, is there?

TSYGANOV. I thought you'd turn out to be some exotic, poisonous flower blooming in the fields of vice, and instead you're just . . . well, what? What are you exactly? What are you looking for? What do you want from life?

LYDIA. When I find out you'll be the first to know.

STEPHAN. This is no place to be looking, that's for sure.

BOGAYEVSKAYA. (*To* TSY.) I hope my presence isn't hindering your eloquence.

TSYGANOV. Not at all. Why do you ask?

BOGAYEVSKAYA. It's just that some people feel shy about using vulgarities in front of a dignified old lady like me . . . it's a pity, really . . .

LYDIA. You're out of touch, Auntie. My friends say things much worse than that.

BOGAYEVSKAYA. Worse? Well, then, apologize. I told you civilization had passed me by.

TSYGANOV. Now now, it's not that bad. (KATYA *comes running in.* STEPAN *jumps up.*)

STEPAN. Well, have you decided?

KATYA. Yes . . . I'll go.

STEPAN. (*Approvingly.*) Good. You won't regret it. (KATYA *goes to* ANNA.)

KATYA. It wasn't easy. He's crying. He looks so helpless.

STEPAN. His just desserts. He's been stepping on people all his life.

KATYA. (*Stamping foot.*) You be quiet. It's none of your business.

TSYGANOV. I'd say it's very much his business. He's the one who swept you away.

ANNA. Now, now, don't be upset. Everything's going to be fine.

KATYA. Nobody swept me away, so you can just stay out of it. It's just . . . I feel sorry for him . . . poor papa

... I love him. I know, I know he's heartless and cruel, but they all are, everyone, even you, Stepan Danilich.

STEPAN. (*Flares up.*) Maybe I am! (*Then laughs.*) Well, the way things are it's hard not to be cruel sometimes.

KATYA. Wipe that grin off your face. I hate it. Just shut up!

ANNA. There, there, Katya, calm down. Let's go into my room. (ANNA *leads* KATYA *to her room.*)

CHERKOON. (*Smile.*) Lively little thing, isn't she?

TSYGANOV. And you, my boy, are about to marry a hornet's nest. (*Enter* STYOPA.)

STYOPA. Stepan Danilich . . .

STEPAN. (*To* TSYGANOV.) I'm getting sick and tired of your sarcasm . . .

CHERKOON. Gentlemen . . . please.

STYOPA. Stepan Danilich . . . Matvey Gogin wants you. (STEPAN *turns abruptly and goes out into the hall followed by* STYOPA.)

TSYGANOV. He has spirit, that boy. Lydia Pavlovna, you're smiling at something?

LYDIA. They make a good couple.

CHERKOON. Oh yes, a fine pair.

LYDIA. I wonder what kind of a life they'll have?

TSYGANOV. A hungry one.

LYDIA. I like him. He has something.

TSYGANOV. He has a smile that says "You're a worm, my friend, you don't exist."

LYDIA. Yes, that's certainly true. (STEPAN *comes in from the hall, smiling slightly, followed by* MATVEY, *dressed in a good new coat. He hesitates, then whispers something in* STEPAN'S *ear.*)

STEPAN. No, no, monsieur, you'll have to say it yourself.

CHERKOON. What is it, Gogin. What do you want?

MATVEY. (*Embarrassed.*) Well, sir, it's like this. You see . . . it's . . . I want to get married, you see . . .

TSYGANOV. That's an original idea. How in the world did you think it up?

MATVEY. Well, sir, it's just . . . it's time, you see. I'm twenty-three.

CHERKOON. Yes. So?

MATVEY. The thing is, sir, er, Yegor Petrovich . . . I need your help. I'll pay you back, I will, sir. See, I know how to get to the peasants, I know what they're scared of cause I'm one myself, so if you ever need me to get round them, just say the word. . . .

STEPAN. See what you've turned out . . . A true man of the people, loyal to his own, selfless and dedicated. (*Enter* KATYA *and* ANNA *who stand by the piano.*)

CHERKOON. What kind of help did you want?

MATVEY. Well, sir, it's Styopa, she's the one I want but she doesn't want me . . . 'never', that's what she said, and that's that. But she's a good girl, she's obedient, she wouldn't fight, you see, if she was married to me she'd be too afraid to talk back so . . . I want to ask if you and the lady wouldn't mind putting a scare into her.

CHERKOON. What for?

MATVEY. So she'll marry me, that's what I'm saying. You tell her she has to, tell her you'll send her back to her father if she doesn't . . . she's scared to death of him. And I've got him all taken care of, gave him fifty copeks already so he'll hand her right over to me, all legal.

KATYA. (*Amazed.*) You pig.

MATVEY. What?

CHERKOON. (*Coldly, to* STEPAN.) Give him his wages. . . .

MATVEY. That's not till the end of the week, sir . . .

CHERKOON. Take your pay and get out of here.
MATVEY. What did I do . . . ?
STEPAN. Think about it.
CHERKOON. Go on, get out.
MATVEY. (*Kneeling.*) Yegor Petrovich . . .
CHERKOON. (*Sharply.*) That's enough.
MATVEY. (*Jumping up.*) But . . . Sergei Nikolayich, what did I do?
KATYA. Hah!
MATVEY. (*Plaintively.*) I'm a good worker. Stepan Danilich, do something, you got me into this.
TSYGANOV. Go on . . . for now. Later, we'll see.
CHERKOON. (*Calmly.*) Later we'll see nothing.
MATVEY. (*Exiting with* STEPAN.) But, sir, you can't just let me go for no good reason . . . it's not fair.
TSYGANOV. (*To* CHERKOON.) That wasn't very smart, Georges, not at all. He's already stolen enough to be satisfied, why go and fire him now? He's not stupid, you know, and anybody smart enough to be a good worker's going to end up stealing sooner or later. (STYOPA *runs in and throws herself at* CHERKOON'S *feet.*)
STYOPA. Yegor Petrovich, god bless you . . .
CHERKOON. What are you doing? Come on, get up.
STYOPA. I was sure you were going to let him have me. I thought for sure you'd give me away.
KATYA. Stupid girl . . .
ANNA. Styopa, listen, please. No one can give you away. You don't belong to anyone. You're no one's property.
STYOPA. (*Fearfully.*) That's just it, I'm all alone, anyone can do anything they want with me. They'll come back, him and my father, they'll take me away. . .
ANNA. (*Going to her.*) That's enough, Styopa.
STYOPA. I'll go to the convent. I will. That's the only

place that's safe. They'll never be able to get me there. They couldn't, could they?

ANNA. Come to my room. (ANNA *takes* STYOPA *to her room.*)

KATYA. (*To* CHERKOON.) You did the right thing, he deserved it. One, two . . . Bang him on the head and kick him out the door.

CHERKOON. Now I know what I have to do to win your approval.

TSYGANOV. (*Yawns.*) So anxiously pursued for all these months.

CHERKOON. But when I dealt with papa Redozubov the same way . . . one, two . . .

KATYA. Oh . . . you! That's different! That's papa! (KATYA *runs into* ANNA'S *room.* ANNA *comes out past her, pours a glass of water and starts back into her room.*)

ANNA. You did the right thing, Yegor.

CHERKOON. (*Frowning.*) Anna, just leave it.

TSYGANOV. That's it, Georges, the humble hero. It suits you.

LYDIA. And you see, Uncle Serge, he's crowned with laurels minutes after the deed is done.

ANNA. (*Exiting.*) Don't you people ever get tired of laughing at everything.

CHERKOON. You think I don't see through all this?

LYDIA. (*Listening.*) Wasn't that the bell?

CHERKOON. (*Quickly.*) Yes, I'll get it. (*Exits.*)

TSYGANOV. And guess who he's hoping it is.

LYDIA. You're very quiet, Auntie.

BOGAYEVSKAYA. I can't think and talk at the same time. I have a problem here.

TSYGANOV. . . . and guess who he's hoping it is . . .

BOGAYEVSKAYA. I seem to be missing a nine, and this deck has five queens in it.

LYDIA. Here's the nine. And that's not a queen, it's a jack.

BOGAYEVSKAYA. Bless my soul, so it is. No wonder. I'm blind as a bat. Now then, little jack, we'll just put you right here . . .

TSYGANOV. (*Singing.*) . . . guess who he's hoping/guess who he's hoping/guess who he's hoping it is . . . (*Singing.*)

LYDIA. Uncle Serge, it wasn't funny the first time and it isn't funny now. Are you almost finished, Auntie? You know it's bad for you to stay up too long.

BOGAYEVSKAYA. In a minute . . . I'll just . . . be . . . a minute. (*Enter* CHERKOON *with* CHIEF OF POLICE.)

CHERKOON. So, you still haven't found Drobyazgin?

CHIEF OF POLICE. (*Gloomily.*) Not a trace. God knows where he could have got to from here. There's no place to go. Good evening, Lydia Pavlovna. Good evening Tatiana Nikolayevna. (*He shakes* TSYGANOV's *hand in silence.*)

BOGAYEVSKAYA. (*Without looking at him.*) So this clerk of yours ran off?

CHIEF OF POLICE. Disappeared . . . into the blue. Scoundrel. We're looking everywhere . . . I'm parched . . .

TSYGANOV. Ah, now I think we can help you there. (*Pours wine.*) How much did he get away with?

CHIEF OF POLICE. That's the most stupid thing of all. He takes four hundred sixty-three roubles and thirty two copeks. There's eight thousand roubles in the safe . . . why didn't he take all of it? Did he think we wouldn't notice?! And what's he have to run away for? It's not murder. Why not just come forward, "Here I am. I did it," he'd get off light, but no, he has to go and hide and I have to pay nine men to flush him out.

CHERKOON. Poor little fool.

BOGAYEVSKAYA. (*Without looking up.*) And he stole

like a beggar . . . in copeks.

TSYGANOV. Spoken like a true thief, Tatiana Nikolayevna. (LYDIA *and* CHERKOON *laugh. The* CHEIF OF POLICE *looks at his watch.*)

CHIEF OF POLICE. Well, you see, the reason I came by, Sergei Nikolayich . . . it's just routine, you understand . . . but the fact of the matter is that you saw him on the day of the crime so I'll have to ask you to . . . well, you know what I mean.

TSYGANOV. (*Mock solemn.*) I understand. I'm suspected of being an accomplice to the crime.

CHIEF OF POLICE. What? Oh, you got me that time. (*Laughs.*) Why can't I just sit and relax with you, that's what I'd like to know. Ah, well, duty calls . . . some damn fool's been reported beating his wife . . .

BOGAYEVSKAYA. (*Not looking up.*) To death?

CHIEF OF POLICE. So it seems. Where's Pritikin? He was just with me. We were going to get up a game of whist . . .

CHERKOON. He's just with Stepan Lukin.

CHIEF OF POLICE. Ah, yes, there's your boy Lukin . . . You ought to have a word with him . . . tell him to watch himself . . . people are getting nervous, you know, say he's been meeting up with the factory workers, putting ideas in their head. He should be a little more careful. Otherwise, well, you know that man Pavlin, oh a very pious and loyal man, poison to the toes, he sees everything . . . even your dreams . . . hate to say it but he even has me fidgity . . . never know who he might be writing to, so I have to act on what he says . . . I wouldn't want to have to . . . to take certain measures. I don't like to make trouble.

TSYGANOV. I understand. I'll take care of it. After all, we don't want to be troubled with trouble.

CHIEF OF POLICE. Exactly! So, farewell one and all. Sergei Nikolayich, you're all right, you know, I like you, I really do.

TSYGANOV. (*Escorting him out.*) Despite the fact that I may well be Porfiry Drobyazgin's accomplice in the dastardly theft of thirty two copeks from this town's vast treasury. (*The* CHIEF OF POLICE *roars with laughter.* PRITIKIN'S *sugary voice can be heard from the hallway, and also the caustic replies of* STEPAN.)

CHERKOON. (*Queitly, to* LYDIA.) Isn't that incredible.

LYDIA. You mean Lukin and the workers?

CHERKOON. No, no, I expected that. But that pathetic little clerk . . . Drobyazgin . . . damnit, we have to do something for him. It really is Sergei's fault, you know. When you come right down to it, he's responsible.

LYDIA. (*Smiles.*) You're not turning respectable on us, are you?

CHERKOON. (*Seriously.*) But you see what I mean, don't you. It was Sergei who put ideas like that in his head. What are you laughing at?

LYDIA. You. I was just remembering the time you said you wanted to turn this town on its head.

CHERKOON. Did I? Well, maybe I did. What brought that up?

LYDIA. Just thought I'd remind you. What was it . . . you said that by willpower alone you'd bring new ideas and new dreams to the people. Uncle Sergei said nothing at all. And look what happened. Not a new idea in sight, but Sergei's managed to leave a trail of corpses behind him.

CHERKOON. Yes, I see what you mean. And so?

LYDIA. Nothing. It's just that none of the good things seem to rub off. And you've grown a little tarnished yourself, Yegor.

STEPHAN. (*From the hallway.*) Yegor Petrovich, would you come here a minute, I need you.

PRITYKIN. (*Off—Protesting.*) Please . . . Yegor Petrovich!

CHERKOON. (*Going out.*) I'll think about that. We'll talk later. (*Exits.*)

LYDIA. Why don't you give up, Auntie. It's time for you to go upstairs. Come on.

BOGAYEVSKAYA. But I feel so at home down here. Wait a minute . . . I just had it . . . now I'm all mixed up again . . . black nine, red ten . . . no, red ten on the . . . on the top pile . . . you know, this is really a most difficult game of solitaire . . .

LYDIA. I'm going up. (*She exits into the hallway and up the stairs.*)

BOGAYEVSKAYA. (*Concentrating on the cards.*) You're going up . . . You're going up . . . And what do I do? Well, now I don't know what I can do? (*She raises her head and looks around.*) Eh? They've all gone. I'm on my own. Ah well, alone, alone, alone. (*She looks at the cards and with a sudden genture mixes them all together.*) Tatiana, my dear, you'll soon be dead. Oh yes, you old fool, quite dead. (*She goes towards the hall.* PELAGEYA *appears in the doorway with a scarf on her head, pathetic-looking, her face flabby, with none of her usual makeup.* BOGAYEVSKAYA *steps back from her.*) What do you want? Who is it?

PELAGEYA. (*Softly.*) It's me . . .

BOGAYEVSKAYA. Pelageya? Oh, it's you.

PELAGEYA. Yes. Is my husband here?

BOGAYEVSKAYA. I think so, yes. Why?

PELAGEYA. (*Weeping.*) He's deserting me. He's never home any more. He spends every evening at Vesyolkina's playing cards with the old man. All he really wants is her, he's just waiting for his chance. . . .

BOGAYEVSKAYA. Don't be silly, your husband couldn't seduce a dragonfly, now stop acting like a fool. Come up to my room and we'll have some tea.

PELAGEYA. Oh, dear Tatiana, you don't know him. Everyone thinks he's so nice, but at home . . . he beats me . . . he does! "You're an ugly old witch" he says, "You've ruined my life, get out of the house," he yells. "I can't stand the sight of you." But where can I go? I have nothing left . . . nothing. I signed everything over to him . . . the house . . . the property. What do I do now? What do I do?

BOGAYEVSKAYA. (*Walking out into hallway.*) You can come upstairs. It's no use making all this racket down here, it won't help.

PELAGEYA. (*Following.*) I'm coming, I'm coming, but tell me what to do about him. What's going to happen to me. Oh dear, I can hear his voice. He's here! Quick, let me go in front of you . . . (*They disappear. At almost the same moment a door opens and is slammed shut.* PRITIKIN *appears from the hall, very agitated, followed by* CHERKOON *and* STEPAN, *carrying the account books.*)

PRITYKIN. Oh, no. No, no, no, my clever little friend, you can't do that to me. Do you know who I am? I'm an important man in this town. I'm known. I'm going to be mayor one day, yes, that's right . . . mayor. And what are you, tell me that? What gives you the right . . . !

CHERKOON. Why don't we just calm down for a moment.

PRITYKIN. Calm down? He called me a swindler. He looked me right in the face and accused me of criminal behavior.

STEPAN. (*Mocking.*) The figures are right here.

PRITYKIN. Oh, yes, figures. I know about figures. You can make them prove anything you want.

STEPAN. Which is exactly what you tried to do, isn't it, except you somehow managed to overlook some thirteen hundred roubles, and we'd like to know where they went?

PRITYKIN. Yego Petrovich, I'm sorry, but I haven't really got time now to be explaining the fundamentals of bookkeeping to a . . . a . . . let's just keep this between us, what do you say? Sergei Nikolayich knows I can be trusted . . . as for Mr. Lukin here, what he wants out of all this I haven't the faintest idea. . . .

STEPAN. I want to catch you cheating.

PRITYKIN. Cheating! I've had enough of these accusations . . .

CHERKOON. Let's leave it till tomorrow.

PRITYKIN. No, sir, I refuse to do that. I'm an honest man, I want this business cleared up, now. Ask Sergei Nikolayich. He checked the books. My calculations were correct, ask him.

CHERKOON. (*Quietly, angrily.*) All right, that's enough. Come in here.

PRITYKIN. Now wait a minute . . . you can't push me around like that . . . (CHERKOON *pushes him through the door of his room and slams it behind them.* STEPAN *throws the account books on the table, thrusts his hands into his pockets and goes out, muttering through his teeth* . . .)

STEPAN. They're all in it together . . . (STYOPA *comes in from* ANNA'S *room with a book in her hands and goes through into the drawing room.* ANNA'S *voice can be heard, reading. Footsteps and noise in the hall. Enter* TSYGANOV *and* NADIEZHDA.)

TSYGANOV. . . . so I decided to go out on the porch, just to be by myself for a while.

NADIEZHDA. Where is everybody?

BARBARIANS

TSYGANOV. (*Slight smile.*) The one you're thinking of will appear when he hears your voice. But he'll give you nothing. Have you noticed how the clouds sweep across the sky, towering black clouds like . . .

NADIEZHDA. I don't care for black. Red is the only important color. Queens always wear red. It's a noble color.

TSYGANOV. My dear, I'll be leaving soon, you know.

NADIEZHDA. And not just you.

TSYGANOV. No, that's right. Wait. Do you mean . . . have you decided?

NADIEZHDA. Decided what?

TSYGANOV. (*Quietly.*) Are you going to come with me? To Paris? Think of it . . . Paris! Barons, countesses . . . all in red from head to toe. I'll give you everything you ever wanted, I promise. I'll give you everything.

NADIEZHDA. (*Calmly.*) Sergei Nikolayich, you're being extremely vulgar. You know I'm not that kind of woman . . .

TSYGANOV. You're wonderful, you're extraordinary, you're terrifying and I love you like I've never loved anyone since I was a young man. Nadiezhda, Nadiezhda, Nadiezhda, we'll be so happy in Paris, you and I, the things we'll do together . . .

NADIEZHDA. Now stop talking like that Sergei Nikolayich. How can you possibly love like a young man when you're almost fifty. In a couple of years you'll be completely bald. Paris this, Paris that . . . what's the point of all this talk when I don't love you. You're an interesting man, and I'm glad I made your acquaintance, but you're too old for me, it's not a good match. It's even . . . you'll forgive me for saying this . . . but it's a little insulting, these ideas you have about me.

TSYGANOV. (*Almost a moan.*) Oooh . . . to hell with

it, we'll get married then, is that better? I'll arrange for you to get a divorce. . . .

NADIEZHDA. It won't make any difference, don't you see? It's the man that's important. All these other things, they don't matter. No more, please. I've learned a lot from you . . . I'm cleverer now . . . I'm a little braver . . .

TSYGANOV. (*Recovering his composure.*) Yes, yes, all right, let's forget it. It's forgotten. I've made my last assault, I promise. It's too late anyway. I haven't got the time . . . or the strength . . .

NADIEZHDA. That's better. You're a wise man, you know. You understand that strength isn't something you can just buy in a shop.

TSYGANOV. Very true, very true . . . it's like tact, which you can't buy anywhere.

NADIEZHDA. Exactly. Now you see it. (*Enter* REDOZUBOV *and* PAVLIN. REDOZUBOV *has aged markedly.*)

REDOZUBOV. Evening. Is my daughter here?

TSYGANOV. I believe so. (*He knocks on* ANNA's *door.*)

REDOZUBOV. (*To* PAVLIN.) You see? In pairs, all of them, oh yes. (ANNA *appears in her doorway.*)

ANNA. Ah, Vassily Ivanich, good evening. Katya.

NADIEZHDA. Good evening, Anna Fyodor'na.

ANNA. Oh . . . *you're* here.

NADIEZHDA. Yes.

KATYA. (*To her father.*) Why do you keep following me around?

PAVLIN. (*Quietly.*) He's worried about you.

ANNA. (*Calling.*) Styopa. (*To* NADIEZHDA.) Would you like some tea?

NADIEZHDA. If it's no trouble. (*Enter* STYOPA.)

ANNA. Bring some tea, Styopa. I'll be right back. (ANNA *goes back into her room.*)

TSYGANOV. And Styopa . . . a little cognac . . . (*He goes up to* NADIEZHDA *and says something to her softly.*)

REDOZUBOV. (*To* KATYA.) Who's in there, just her?

KATYA. Who else?

REDOZUBOV. You know.

KATYA. Stop it, papa. I'm not a baby.

REDOZUBOV. Come home, Katya. Please. You'll be gone in a few days. You could at least spend them at home with me, eh? I know I'll never see you again.

KATYA. All right. Wait here. I'll just be a minute. (*She goes quickly into* ANNA'S *room.*)

REDOZUBOV. (*To* PAVLIN.) See that? She doesn't want to know me any more. They took my daughter away . . . made my son an alcoholic and what happens to them? Nothing at all.

PAVLIN. Don't worry. Just wait.

REDOZUBOV. Wait? Wait for what? Who can I go to?

PAVLIN. They can buy the Chief of Police, but they can't buy the lord almighty. Their time will come.

REDOZUBOV. They coddle that Pritikin and they butcher me. Now they have my daughter. She's in there with them. That student might be in there with her right this minute, and here I am, waiting. Me. Redozubov. (*Jumps up, bellowing.*) KATYA!!!!

NADIEZHDA. My god, what's that?

TSYGANOV. My dear Mr. Mayor, what seems to be the trouble? (*Enter* CHERKOON *with* PRITIKIN, *who looks like he has a toothache.* KATYA *and* ANNA *come running in.*)

KATYA. What are you yelling about?

REDOZUBOV. Katya . . . get home.

CHERKOON. Keep it down. What do you think this is, a cattle auction?

REDOZUBOV. Go ahead . . . go on, beat me to death. Thief. Go on, finish me off, what are you waiting for?

KATYA. Papa, please . . .

CHERKOON. Listen, old man . . .

REDOZUBOV. Silence. Don't you dare talk to me like that, you . . . you anacrist, you . . . Go home Katerina. Now! Well, Pritikin, happy now? Pleased with yourself? Jackel. Scavenger.

PRITYKIN. Vassily Ivanich, it's not my fault, I swear . . .

REDOZUBOV. Ha! Listen to him. Marries a rich old woman, robs her blind . . . and what now . . . a mistress is it . . . what else, mayor of the town, is that what you're thinking about, is that what comes next, parasite, leech, cockroach, bloodsucker . . .

CHERKOON. Would you two please take this fight somewhere else.

KATYA. (*Shouting.*) Stop it, papa, you'll make them throw you out. I'd be so ashamed if they did that . . . I'd never be able to come back here and then I'd hate you . . .

REDOZUBOV. What?

ANNA. She loves you, don't you see that? She's been crying her poor heart out in there. Believe me, she loves you very much.

REDOZUBOV. Then why's she leaving me?

KATYA. Please, please, papa, for god's sake, let's go home. (KATYA *leads her father into the hall.* PAVLIN *makes a peculiar move towards the door and then stands there, listening.*)

CHERKOON. You'd better go, too, Pritikin. We're done talking.

PRITYKIN. (*Sighing.*) I'll go. I'll go. But I won't forget

that student in a hurry . . . oh no. He's from this town . . . and so am I. And there's things I know. (PRITIKIN *exits.*)

ANNA. My god this is all so strange. (NADIEZHDA *has been watching* CHERKOON *from the corner, her face fixed in a strange smile.* TSYGANOV *smokes furiously at his cigar and looks at everyone, twitching his moustache.* STYOPA *prepares the tea and looks furtively at* PAVLIN *with hatred in her eyes.* ANNA *looks at* NADIEZHDA, *shudders, makes a move towards her, then turns quickly and goes into her room.*)

TSYGANOV. (*To* CHERKOON.) Have you . . . worked everything out with Pritikin?

CHERKOON. Yes. And I think you and I better have a little talk. Oh, Nadiezhda Polikarpovna, hello. Didn't see you there.

TSYGANOV. Obviously we're not going to have our little talk now.

CHERKOON. No, I suppose not. (*To* NADIEZHDA.) What are you doing hiding in the shadows? Why don't we go into the drawing room.

NADIEZHDA. I'd love to go into the drawing room. I was just waiting to see when you'd notice me. (*They go into the drawing room. Their voices can be heard in quiet conversation.*)

TSYGANOV. (*To* PAVLIN.) Still here, eh? Something on you mind? Well?

PAVLIN. If I may be allowed, sir . . . have you had a chance to look through my essay? I was curious to know what you thought of it. (TSYGANOV *looks at him in silence,* PAVLIN *backs away.*) The little notebook . . . the manuscript of my work. I was asking if by any chance you'd had a moment to read it.

TSYGANOV. What? Oh, yes, that. (*Brusquely.*) It's

complete trash.

PAVLIN. (*Incredulously.*) My work . . . my nine years of labor . . . trash?

TSYGANOV. (*Scornfully.*) I'll go find this philosophical landmark of yours. (TSYGANOV *exits.*)

PAVLIN. I saw your father again today, young lady. (STYOPA *leans her hands on the table and stares at him.*) Freezing wind . . . drizzle, and there he was, limping along, a little drunk and weeping, weeping bitterly . . .

STYOPA. (*In a low vioce.*) You're a liar. Stop trying to make me feel bad. (*She throws the samovar lid at him.*) There, take that, you demon . . . evil-eye . . . (ANNA *runs in from her room.*)

ANNA. What was that? (PAVLIN *picks up the lid.*)

PAVLIN. The lid fell off. An accident.

STYOPA. Make him leave! (TSYGANOV *comes in with* PAVLIN's *notebook.*)

TSYGANOV. Here you are.

STYOPA. Order him out of here.

PAVLIN. *Order me.* You won't have to do that, I assure you. I leave of my own free volition. (ANNA *goes to* STYOPA *and asks something quietly.* STYOPA *exits into* ANNA's *room.* ANNA *stands by the table, hears the conversation in the drawing room. Her face shows pain and revulsion.*)

PAVLIN. So you've made up your mind that my work is . . . trash.

TSYGANOV. Yes, yes.

PAVLIN. In other words, for nine years, for nine whole years my thinking has been misguided. Thank you for that information. I'm deeply indebted to you. Of course there's no chance at all that you might be completely mistaken. Good day. (PAVLIN *exits.*)

TSYGANOV. The Chief of Police was right. He *is* poison. Are you feeling all right?

BARBARIANS 115

ANNA. (*Whispering.*) What's she saying? Listen.

TSYGANOV. At times like this I find my hearing becomes mysteriously impared.

ANNA. My god, what does she think she's doing?

TSYGANOV. (*Loudly.*) Tea's ready. Let's all have some tea!

CHERKOON. Be right with you.

ANNA. (*Softly, with pain.*) I wasn't eavesdropping, you know.

TSYGANOV. I didn't say a word.

ANNA. That's what you think, isn't it. You should be ashamed of yourself.

TSYGANOV. No . . . really . . . (ANNA *runs off into her room.*) Yegor, come here a moment, would you. (CHERKOON *appears in the doorway.*)

CHERKOON. What is it?

TSYGANOV. (*Quietly.*) Listen, your wife just heard something in there. She was very upset.

CHERKOON. Same old story. It's nothing, really. Nadiezhda Polikarpovna on her favorite subject. She's telling me how different people declare their love. She's completely out of her mind, you know. It's quite funny. (*He goes out quickly.* TSYGANOV *shrugs, twiddles his moustache, pours out a huge glass of cognac and drinks it down. He picks up his hat and goes into the hall.* MONAKHOV *comes to meet him, subdued and sad.*)

MONAKHOV. (*Softly.*) Evening.

TSYGANOV. Oh . . . hello. Some cognac?

MONAKHOV. Please. Terrible weather, isn't it? Is my Nadiezhda here?

TSYGANOV. (*Pours.*) A little more? (MONAKHOV *nods in silence.* TSYGANOV *whistles a tune.*)

MONAKHOV. (*Softly.*) I came to get her.

TSYGANOV. (*Smiling.*) Do you want me to call her?

MONAKHOV. No . . . I don't . . . not yet. Let me have

another drink first.

TSYGANOV. (*Smiling.*) You think that'll make it easier?

MONAKHOV. Don't laugh. It isn't funny, you know.

TSYGANOV. Don't you remember our little bet?

MONAKHOV. Yes. You lost.

TSYGANOV. So you should be happy. Hey, what's the matter? Please, none of that.

MONAKHOV. (*Weeping.*) I'm sorry . . . it hurts . . . what do I do now . . . what can I do . . . she's all I have. Without her . . . nothing. I've got nothing. (TSYGANOV *tries to conceal his discomfort.*)

TSYGANOV. Come on now, that's enough. Look, let's go to my room . . . or we can go for a walk, anything, but don't . . . if you have to suffer, fine, but for god's sake don't make yourself ridiculous. Dignity, my friend, dignity at all costs. (*They go out into the hall. The room is quiet except for the soft, purring words of* NADIEZHDA *from the drawing room.*)

NADIEZHDA. True love is when you've no regrets, when you're never afraid.

CHERKOON. (*Laugh.*) Well, that's enough of that. You seem particularly inspired today. (CHERKOON *appears in the drawing room doorway. He is excited.*)

NADIEZHDA. (*Behind him.*) No, but what I'm saying is that love is something you can't really talk about. I was only telling you how certain people declare their love, but love itself, real love only happens in silence.

CHERKOON. (*Mutters.*) In silence, eh? Well, let's have some tea . . . in silence.

NADIEZHDA. (*Softly.*) You're afraid, aren't you?

CHERKOON. Afraid? Afraid of what?

NADIEZHDA. Me. I never expected that from you . . .

CHERKOON. Look, that's enough, really . . .

BARBARIANS

NADIEZHDA. I thought you weren't afraid of anything.

CHERKOON. (*Standing close to her.*) Be careful, Nadiezhda . . .

NADIEZHDA. Why? Why should I be careful. I'm not afraid. (CHERKOON *puts his hands on her shoulders.*)

CHERKOON. You . . . you're in love with me, aren't you? Go ahead, say it . . . you love me, right?

NADIEZHDA. (*Quietly, firmly.*) Yes. The first time I saw you, and ever since. Georges . . . you're my Georges, aren't you? (*She embraces him suddenly. He makes a move to free himself.* ANNA *enters. She's been crying and has a handkerchief in her hands. She sees* CHERKOON *and* NADIEZHDA, *draws herself up, tense as a spring.*)

ANNA. Stop it . . . don't . . .

CHERKOON. (*With a drunken smile.*) No, no, no, Anna, it's not what you think. Although it doesn't really matter either way now.

NADIEZHDA. Yes. Now. It doesn't matter.

ANNA. You're disgusting . . . you're repulsive . . .

NADIEZHDA. (*Calmly.*) Because I love him?

CHERKOON. (*As if just waking up.*) Anna, wait. Just be quiet for a moment.

ANNA. Be quiet! God, how low can you stoop. Why her?! The other I could understand, but . . . this . . . this thing . . . this animal . . .

NADIEZHDA. (*To* CHERKOON.) Please take me out, Georges . . .

CHERKOON. Wait a minute. Now listen to me, Nadiezhda . . . (*Noises from the hallway.* TSYGANOV *comes running in, pursued by the* DOCTOR, MONAKHOV *behind.*)

TSYGANOV. Hold him down, grab him. (*The* DOCTOR

has a large, old fashioned revolver. He steadies himself with one hand on the door hinge and aims at TSYGANOV.)

DR. MAKAROV. I'm going to kill you. I'm going to kill you. (*He fires, misses, but grazes* TSYGANOV's *finger.*)

TSYGANOV. Damn fool, can't even shoot straight. (CHERKOON *rushes to the* DOCTOR.)

CHERKOON. Give it to me. Give it here.

ANNA AND NADIEZHDA. (*Together.*) No, Yegor . . . he'll kill you . . . get away from him . . . (*The* DOCTOR *turns the revolver chamber with his fingers. It's stuck.*)

DR. MAKAROV. God damnit . . . turn . . . turn . . . (NADIEZHDA *grabs the gun from him.*)

NADIEZHDA. You stupid fool.

CHERKOON. Are you crazy?

MONAKHOV. Nadya, put the gun down, put it down. (LYDIA *runs in from upstairs.*)

LYDIA. What's going on?

TSYGANOV. (*Agitated.*) That's all I need. I have enough sins of my own without paying for others people's. You savage.

ANNA. (*To* LYDIA.) He was kissing that . . . that thing. (*To* MONAKHOV.) Get her out of here. (*To* LYDIA.) They were kissing. I saw them. . . . (LYDIA *leads* ANNA *into her room.*)

LYDIA. Styopa, ask my aunt to come down, would you. (STYOPA *runs out into the hallway and disappears up the stairs.*)

DR. MAKAROV. (*In a low voice, to* CHERKOON.) Kissing? You?

CHERKOON. Get out. (TSYGANOV *is wrapping a handkerchief around his hand.*)

TSYGANOV. Ah, at last he's seen the light.

DR. MAKAROV. (*Miserably.*) Nadiezhda! Have you

chosen? (NADIEZHDA *has been staring at the* DOCTOR *with a triumphant smile.*)

NADIEZHDA. Yes. I've chosen him. (*She points with pride towards* CHERKOON.)

MONAKHOV. (*Groaning.*) No . . . no, Nadya . . . Nadiusha . . . why? (BOGAYEVSKAYA *enters, followed by* STYOPA, *crosses to* ANNA'S *room without stopping.*)

BOGAYEVSKAYA. So it's come to this, eh, murder and mayhem in my own house. (*Exits.*)

DR. MAKAROV. (*To* TSYGANOV.) So . . . it wasn't you after all. My apologies. So he's the one. I should have . . . never mind, you're all the same anyway. Vultures. I'm sorry I didn't kill the pair of you. Yes, I'm sorry.

NADIEZHDA. (*Sympathetically.*) You couldn't have. You can't really do anything . . .

DR. MAKAROV. That's right. What can I do? Nothing. I'm useless.

CHERKOON. Please everybody, that's enough of this.

MONAKHOV. Nadya, please, come home.

NADIEZHDA. (*Firmly.*) This is my home now. Here. Wherever he (CHERKOON.) is.

DR. MAKAROV. For four long years my heart's been on fire. Now what do I do . . . what?!

TSYGANOV. Shut up. Nobody's interested. You shot my fingernail off. Why don't you just leave.

CHERKOON. (*To* DOC.) Yes, you're getting off lightly for that little escapade. Just go now and we'll forget the whole thing.

DR. MAKAROV. (*Coming to himself, simply.*) Good-bye, Nadiezhda. I love you. Forgive me . . . for everything . . . good-bye. He'll ruin you, he will, you'll see. Good-bye. Good-bye, vultures. (*The* DOCTOR *exits.*)

TSYGANOV. (*To* NADIEZHDA.) Well, I hope you're

happy now. It's just like in all the best novels. One happy love story, three or four tragic ones . . . an attempted murder . . . a gunshot . . . blood . . . (*Shows his wrapped finger.*) . . . wonderful.

NADIEZHDA. What'll he do now? Do you think he'll try to kill himself?

TSYGANOV. He should. I mean I would . . . out of sheer embarrassment.

MONAKHOV. (*Quietly, to* CHERKOON.) Give me back my wife. Give her back. She's all I have . . . she's everything to me . . . I've given my whole life . . . my whole life . . .

CHERKOON. Take her. Please. She's yours.

NADIEZHDA. (*Amazed, to* CHERKOON.) What? What did you say? You told him to take me?

CHERKOON. (*Firmly.*) Yes. Look, Nadiezhda Polikarpovna . . . I'm sorry, I really am . . .

NADIEZHDA. For what?

CHERKOON. What happened before . . . it didn't mean anything . . . really. I was just . . . for one moment something happened . . . you were being very provocative, you know. Anyway, whatever it was, it wasn't love, believe me.

NADIEZHDA. (*Muffled.*) I don't understand. You have to tell me so I can follow what you're saying.

CHERKOON. I don't love you. Is that clear enough?

NADIEZHDA. (*Incredulous.*) I don't believe you. That can't be true. You kissed me. No one's ever kissed me before, only you . . .

MATVEY. But Nadiezhda, what about me . . .

NADIEZHDA. Be quiet. You don't exist.

CHERKOON. Please everyone can we get this over with. I don't love you. I'm sorry, and that's all there is to it.

NADIEZHDA. (*With a mysterious sadness.*) No . . . no

... Look, I'll sit down, you sit next to me and we'll talk. Georges, sit down . . . sit right here, all right? Please. Yegor Petrovich?

CHERKOON. I don't love you. I don't love you. I don't love you. (CHERKOON *goes into his room.* NADIEZHDA *sits down on the sofa, stunned.* TSYGANOV *is amazed and delighted. His moustache twitching.* MONAKHOV *stands by the door looking broken.*)

TSYGANOV. (*Cheerfully.*) This must be the most topsy-turvy town in all of Russia. The doctor's supposed to cure people; instead, he shoots them . . .

MONAKHOV. Nadya . . . !

NADIEZHDA. Mmmmm?

MONAKHOV. Let's go home.

NADIEZHDA. (*Calmly, softly.*) Go yourself. You don't exist. Go away, Dead man. (MONAKHOV, *with a sigh, goes out into the hallway.*)

TSYGANOV. (*Quietly.*) There's still Paris, if you're interested. Are you?

NADIEZHDA. He doesn't love me, does he. It's true, isn't it.

TSYGANOV. Obviously. Anyone who really loved you would . . .

NADIEZHDA. Don't. I know.

TSYGANOV. So that's that. Nadiezhda . . .

NADIEZHDA. (*Sadly.*) Maybe he's just afraid.

TSYGANOV. (*Sighing.*) What's he got to be afraid of?

NADIEZHDA. The Doctor . . . will he try to kill himself do you think?

TSYGANOV. I doubt it. But then again, maybe. And if so, so what? Aren't you used to it by now? Yesterday the statistician, today the Doctor, tomorrow, perhaps me.

NADIEZHDA. (*Shaking her head.*) He couldn't

anyway. The guns right here.

TSYGANOV. He could buy another one.

NADIEZHDA. They don't sell them in town. God, it's stuffy in here. Let's go out . . . on the porch. I'd like some air.

TSYGANOV. To the porch, to the roof, to the moon, anywhere you say. I love you Nadiezhda, I love you. . . .

NADIEZHDA. (*With deep conviction.*) No, please don't say that. How can you love me if he can't. He was afraid. Even him. No one can ever love me. That's what it is, you see. No one. No-one can love me. Ever. (*They go out.* STYOPA *comes running out of* ANNA's *room, followed by* LYDIA. STYOPA *takes something from a cupboard.* CHERKOON *comes in, glowering, crushed.*)

LYDIA. Fifteen drops, Styopa.

STYOPA. Everything's so mixed up . . . what a life . . .

LYDIA. Hurry . . . hurry . . . (STYOPA *exits back into* ANNA's *room.*)

CHERKOON. How's Anna?

LYDIA. (*Shrugs.*) All right. What do you want me to say?

CHERKOON. I mean, is she . . . it's going to be awkward seeing her.

LYDIA. What exactly are you expecting from her?

CHERKOON. Please . . . would you tell her Nadiezhda Polikarpovna's gone. I tried to explain what happened . . . I asked her to forgive me. She's gone. I'm sure she won't come back now.

LYDIA. I don't understand. What *did* happen?

CHERKOON. She . . . god it's so stupid . . . she was telling me all her silly ideas about love, it was completely innocent . . . but she . . . she was so . . . she has this incredible power somehow . . . she . . . I don't know, I kissed her, that's all, I couldn't help it, it was nothing . . . nothing.

LYDIA. You poor thing. She led you on, she seduced you, it's all her fault.

CHERKOON. (*Quietly.*) You find me quite contemptible right now.

LYDIA. (*Emphatically, vengefully.*) Oh yes . . . yes I do, I find you contemptible, I find you pathetic and revolting.

CHERKOON. Lydia, please . . . I told you I didn't know what was happening to me in this place . . . I admitted it . . .

LYDIA. I'm sorry. I'm not here to rescue anyone. If people are too weak to stand up to circumstances, let them fall, let them rot and be forgotten, we don't need them. We don't need anything inferior and helpless.

CHERKOON. I thought you were . . . I thought you saw something in me . . . I didn't want to disappoint you . . . I admired your strength. Now I'm afraid to tell you . . .

LYDIA. Yes, you're afraid. You're a coward. You had me fooled for a moment. I thought I'd finally found a strong, honest man, someone I could respect. For a long time now I've been looking for someone I could bow down to and walk by his side. Maybe it's impossible, but I'll have nothing less . . .

CHERKOON. Someone you could bow down to . . .

LYDIA. Someone that was worthy of me. I can't believe there aren't people like that . . . somewhere on this earth . . . rare, brilliant people, people with a mission in life, visionaries. Surely they must exist . . . they must . . .

CHERKOON. (*In a muffled, despairing voice.*) Life's too powerful. You try, but you can't hold onto what's best in you. It all gets dragged down into the filth.

LYDIA. It's no excuse. There's greed and filth everywhere, it's no excuse. (*A shot from outside.*)

CHERKOON. (*Miserably.*) Oh god, now what, now

what? (ANNA *rushes in from her room.*)

ANNA. Yegor! I thought . . . what was that? (*She collapses on the sofa.*)

LYDIA. I'll go see. (LYDIA *exits.* BOGAYEVSKAYA *comes in from* ANNA'S *room.*)

BOGAYEVSKAYA. What was that noise? I was about to go up to bed.

TSYGANOV. (*In hallway.*) Don't come out here. Stay inside.

CHERKOON. Who fired the shot? (TSYGANOV *enters. He is pale, his moustache drooping.*)

TSYGANOV. It was her. Nadiezhda Polikarpovna.

CHERKOON. Who did she shoot?

TSYGANOV. (*Shuddering.*) Herself. She shot herself. Right in front of me. And her husband. Just pointed the gun . . . so calm . . . so deliberate . . . it's madness . . . madness. (BOGAYEVSKAYA *goes into the hallway.*)

BOGAYEVSKAYA. Silly woman. I'd never have thought . . . not her. (ANNA *rushes to her husband.*)

ANNA. Yegor, it's not your fault, it's not your fault.

CHERKOON. Where's that damned doctor, someone get him.

MONAKHOV. (*Entering.*) No need for that. No need for anything now. You've killed a human being. Why?

ANNA. Oh, Yegor, it wasn't you. It wasn't.

MONAKHOV. (*Quietly, with horror.*) What have you done? Tell me. What have you done?

(*All are silent. The howling wind can be heard outside.*)

CURTAIN

COSTUME PLOT

IVAKIN (Jerome Dempsey) —
1 pair trousers, 1 pair boots, 1 shirt, 1 apron, 1 hat, 2 pairs socks, 1 set suspenders.

MATVEY (Stephen Lang) —
1 pale green peasant shirt, 1 off white peasant shirt, 1 pair trousers, 2 pairs boots, 1 black vest, 1 belt, 1 embroidered cap, 2 ribbons for boots, 1 jacket, 2 pairs black socks.

YEFIM (Peter Phillips) —
1 Wallace Beery shirt, 1 pair pants, 1 pair boots (to carry only), 1 set suspenders, 1 black cap.

DUNYA'S HUSBAND (Frank Maraden) —
1 baggy pants, 1 silk rag shirt, 1 grey wool vest, leather straps, burlap shoe wraps, 1 pair felt boots, 1 cap, 1 leather pouch (shoulder bag), 1 T-shirt.

MARIA IVANOVNA VESYOLKINA (Sherry Steiner) —
1 petticoat, 1 bustle, 1 corset, 1 body perfector, 1 fuschia bodice, 1 green cotton floral skirt, 1 black leather belt, 1 burgundy velvet belt, 1 black leather reticule, 1 white beaded reticule, 1 chiffon paisley shawl, 1 straw hat, 1 striped parasol, 1 handkerchief, 1 bar pin, earrings, broach, ring, black tights, 1 pair black boots.

DROBYAZGIN (Michael Hammond) —
1 black uniform jacket, 1 black uniform trousers, 1 cap, 1 white shirt, 1 collar, 1 pair boots, 2 pairs socks.

PRITYKIN (Gary Bayer)—
2 shirts, tank top undershirt, 4 collars, 2 sets cufflinks, ring, tie pin, beige spats, button boots, 2 pairs black socks, 1 mustard three-piece cutaway suit with suspenders, 1 tie, 1 ascot, 1 straw boater, 1 two-piece grey suit, 1 cane.

DR. MAKAROV (Bill Moor)—
1 grey three-piece suit, 1 black vest, 1 shirt, 1 pair cufflinks, 2 pairs black socks, 1 black caped overcoat, 1 pair suspenders, 1 straw Panama, 1 black felt fedora, 1 tie, 1 bow tie, 2 collars, 1 pair black shoes, 1 pair brown button shoes, 1 pair boots.

MONAKHOV (Brian Murray)—
2 piece uniform (dark green), 1 brown vest, 2 ties, 1 bow tie, 1 two-piece grey suit, 1 grey vest, 2 pairs suspenders, 2 pairs black socks, 1 pair black shoes, 1 straw hat, 1 black hat, 1 black overcoat, 1 tank top undershirt.

LYDIA (Roxanne Hart)—
2 petticoats, 2 dickies, 1 riding jacket, 1 riding skirt, 1 corset, 1 bustle, 1 green dress, 1 cumberbund, 1 green silk jacket, 1 purple skirt and jacket, 1 blouse, 2 pairs shoes, tights, handkerchief, 2 tie pins, 2 pairs earrings, 2 rings, locket.

NADEZHDA (Sheila Allen)—
1 petticoat, 1 lavender dress with red-green silk sash, tights, 2 pairs shoes, hat, handkerchief, biege linen dress, silk dickie, rope belt, green-blue velvet dress, red silk rose, blue silk cumberbund, white silk parasol, necklace, earrings, ring, broach.

BARBARIANS

PELAGEYA (Joan Pape) —
1 petticoat, 1 waist cincher, 1 bustle, 1 body pefector, 1 mauve skirt, beige and pink striped bodies, purple bodice, grey skirt and blouse, black knee highs, quilted mauve jacket, pink and gold reticule, 2 straw hats, black and white bandanna, 1 pair gloves, cameo pin, 1 "pin watch", lace parasol, cameo on chain, 2 rings, dangle earrings, 2 hat pins, handkerchief, black shoes.

TATYANA NIKOLAYEVNA
BOGAYEVSKAYA (Avril Gentles) —
Padding, 1 corset, 1 petticoat, 4 bodices, 1 black silk shawl with white embroidery, black knee stockings, handkerchief, camisole, black lace gloves, 3 broaches, 2 pairs earrings, 4 rings, pearl locket, black green stone locket, cameo, magnifier, black reticule, grey parasol.

REDOZUBOV (Patrick Hines) —
2 white shirts, 2 collars, 1 three-piece frock coat suit, grey vest, grey peasant shirt, grey peasant overcoat, black top hat, black suspenders, 2 pairs black socks, 1 pair black shoes, 1 ascot.

LUKIN (Boyd Gaines) —
2 shirts, 2 collars, 1 brown vest, 1 pair trousers, 1 belt, 1 union shirt, 1 Russian wool peasant shirt, 1 wool cap, 2 pairs socks, 1 pair shoes, 1 pair riding boots, 1 pair cufflinks.

TSYGANOV (John Seitz) —
1 three-piece linen suit, 1 three-piece brown suit, 2 vests, 2 shirts, 1 straw Panama, 4 collars, 2 handkerchiefs, 1 pair pale green socks, 1 pair dark socks, 1 ascot, 1 tie, 1 bow tie, 2 beige shirts (striped), 1 monocle, 2 sets cuff-

links, 1 tie pin, 1 ring, 1 pair beige shoes, 1 pair black shoes, 2 pairs suspenders, 1 tank top undershirt.

ANNA (Marti Maraden)—
1 petticoat, 1 bustle, 1 beige silk dress with bolero and cumberbund, 1 blue bodice, blue skirt and jacket, 1 dark blue belt and cumberbund, 2 pairs shoes, parasol, 1 pair tights, reticule, handkerchief, gloves, hat, hat pin, 1 pair earrings, ring, wedding band, medallion on chain, cameo.

STYOPA (Anna Kluger Levine)—
1 petticoat, black tights, 1 pair black boots, orange and white print dress with cumberbund, cotton blue and white striped skirt, white cotton blouse, peach blouse with blue trim, 1 breast binder, 1 cotton apron, 1 lace apron, 1 dark blue-green shawl, cross on chain, dark blue wool skirt, hair ribbon.

CHERKOON (Jon Polito)—
1 pair black boots, 2 pairs black socks, 2 shirts, 1 three-piece brown suit, 1 two-piece blue suit, 1 brown vest, 1 belt, 3 ties, 1 pair suspenders, 4 collars, 1 pair black shoes, 2 pairs undershorts.

GRISHA (Michael John McGann)—
Padding, 1 Russian shirt, 1 vest, 1 belt, 1 jacket, 1 overcoat, 1 pair shoes, 2 pairs socks, 1 pair suspenders.

KATYA (Christine Estabrook)—
Red cotton skirt, beige shirt, 1 pair lace-up canvas boots, 1 red scarf, under bloomers, canvas belt, black tights, medallion on chain, 1 petticoat, 1 bustle, 1 cor-

set, 1 body perfector, camisole, 1 pair character shoes, grey blouse, tweed skirt.

CHIEF OF POLICE (Richard Jamieson) —
Uniform jacket and trousers, uniform overcoat, uniform hat, 2 shirts, 1 collar, 1 pair black riding boots, uniform belt, sword, 1 pair black gloves, 1 pair cufflinks, 2 pairs black socks.

PAVLIN (John Heffernan) —
1 black belt, 1 grey silk Russian shirt, rumpled overcoat, grey wool gloves, 1 cap, 2 pairs black socks, 1 pair boots (character should be disheveled.)

PROPERTY PLOT

ACT ONE

Preset onstage
Table — 2' × 6'
2 benches — 5' long
1 bench — 4' long
Stool
Tray with larger beer jug and 6 mugs
Old bucket on rope
Old broom stick
Rustic storage bins with bread, rolls, vegetables, onions, baskets, boxes.
Rough Hessian curtains
Old tattered cloth
Half loaf of dark bread (edible)

Preset offstage
IVAKIN — Guitar, tray with small beer jug and 4 mugs
MATVEY — Bedroll with cross ties
LYDIA — Riding crop
ANNA — Coins, small traveling bag
VESYOLKINA — Flowers
DUNYA'S HUSBAND — Bag
STYOPA — 2 medium suitcases
LUKIN — Duffle bag
OTHER — 4 suitcases, 1 trunk, 15 extra mugs.

ACT TWO

Preset onstage
Geranium pots around tree trunk

BARBARIANS

Cherkoon's table — 2'6" × 5'
Cherkun's chair
Octagonal wicker tea table
3 wicker chairs with light floral cushions
1 wicker rocker
On Cherkoon's table:
  Glass with liquid
  Engineering drawings
  Topographical maps
  Paper
  Pencils
  Compass
  Triangles
  T-square
  Notebook
  Larger book
  Map case
  Ashtray

Preset offstage
STYOPA — Tray with decanter of Port, Chartreuse bottle, liqueur bottle, decanter of vodka, decanter of cognac, brandy glasses, small glasses. Tea basket with 10 glasses, 2 bottles of lemonade, 6 beers, liqueurs, 2 plates with snacks, 2 tablecloths.
MATVEY — Small folder
ANNA — Book
CHERKOON — Coins
MONAKHOV — Cigars, metal case
PAVLIN — Manuscript
KATYA — Small pebbles, 1 large rock, 4 sticks, 1 long stick
TSYGANOV — Cigarettes, gold cigarette case, cigarette holder

ACT THREE

Preset onstage
Furniture — same as Act Two
Small table
6 colored lanterns
6 white lanterns (strung above stage)
1 step ladder (strung above stage)
Flower garlands
Lamplighter's taper
Hurricane lamps
On Cherkoon's table:
    Champagne in cooler
    Wine bottles
    Chartreuse bottle
    Service plates with cheese, pastries, rolls, fish, fruit
    Plates
    Seltzer bottle
    Pears
    Fruit knife

Preset offstage
MONAKHOV — Clarinet
BOGAYEVSKAYA — Handkerchief
LYDIA — 2 page note with envelope
STYOPA — Coins
CHERKOON — Cigarettes, cigarette, matches

ACT FOUR

Preset onstage
Desk with lamp and abacus
Desk chair

BARBARIANS

Bar tabe with 3 wine glasses, wine bottle, water carafe, tumblers, ashtray, vase
Cupboard for medicine box
Round table
Table cover
Candle
2 chairs
Piano with lamp and music score, shawl draped on piano
Piano stool
1 large portrait
2 rectangular landscapes
2 square portraits
Lace curtains
Sconce on wall
Chaise
Rug — 9' × 12'
Arm chair (Covered with white cloth)
Side table with lamp, ashtray
Chandelier
Heavy drapes
Ashtray
Cards
3 account books
3 brandy glasses

Preset offstage
STYOPA — Medicine box with 4 bottles, book, tray with samovar with lid and damper, tea pot, 6 tea glasses
CHIEF OF POLICE — Pocket watch
TSYGANOV — Cigars, matches, Pavlin's manuscript, small tray with cognac glasses, glasses, bloody finger, bloody handkerchief

ANNA — Handkerchief
DR. MAKAROV — Revolver
MONAKHOV — Glasses
PRITYKIN — Walking stick
REDOZUBOV — Walking stick

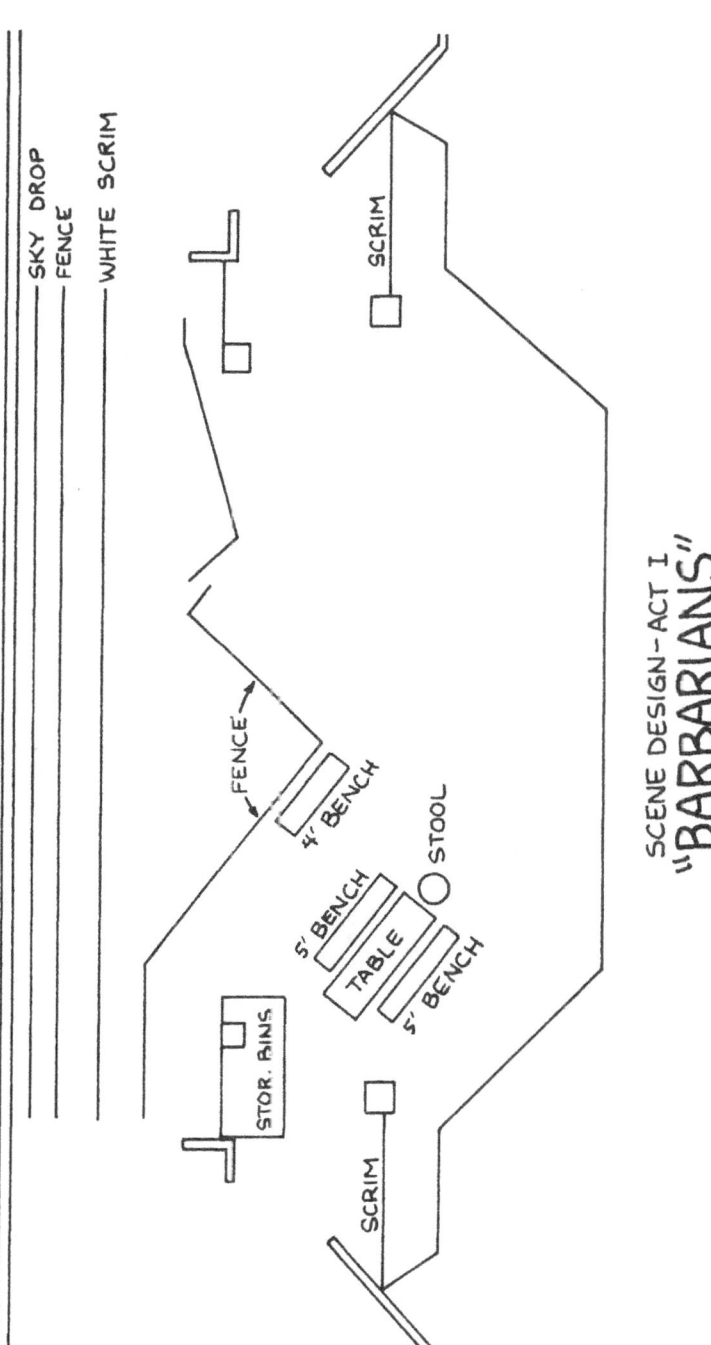

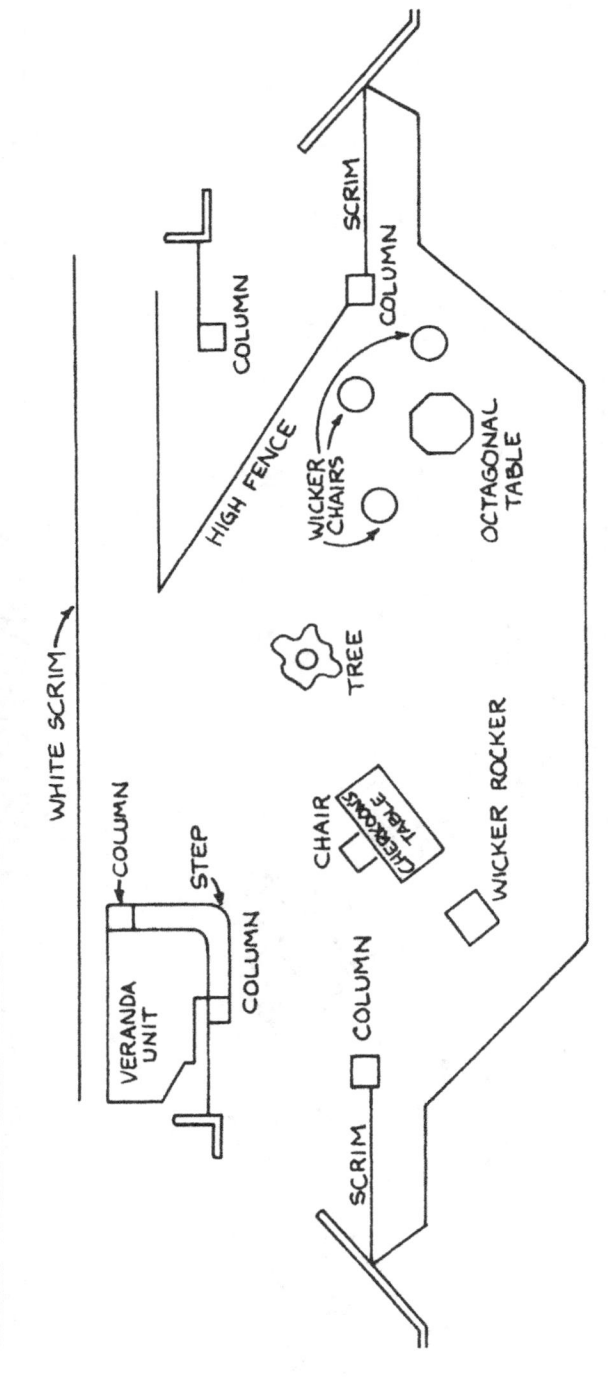

MUSIC USE NOTE

Licensees are solely responsible for obtaining formal written permission from copyright owners to use copyrighted music in the performance of this play and are strongly cautioned to do so. If no such permission is obtained by the licensee, then the licensee must use only original music that the licensee owns and controls. Licensees are solely responsible and liable for all music clearances and shall indemnify the copyright owners of the play(s) and their licensing agent, Samuel French, against any costs, expenses, losses and liabilities arising from the use of music by licensees. Please contact the appropriate music licensing authority in your territory for the rights to any incidental music.

IMPORTANT BILLING AND CREDIT REQUIREMENTS

If you have obtained performance rights to this title, please refer to your licensing agreement for important billing and credit requirements.

www.ingramcontent.com/pod-product-compliance
Lightning Source LLC
Chambersburg PA
CBHW051404290426
44108CB00015B/2143